The Road Not Taken

Two roads diverged in a yellow wood,
And sorry I could not travel both
And be one traveler, long I stood
And looked down one as far as I could
To where it bent in the undergrowth;
Then took the other, as just as fair
And having perhaps the better claim,
Because it was grassy and wanted wear;
Though as for that the passing there
Had worn them really about the same,
And both that morning equally lay
In leaves no step had trodden black.
Oh, I kept the first for another day!
Yet knowing how way leads on to way
I doubted if I should ever come back.
I shall be telling this with a sigh
Somewhere ages and ages hence:
Two roads diverged in a wood, and I --
I took the one less traveled by,
And that has made all the difference.

– Robert Frost

Table of Contents

Before You Begin...

Did you know that the decisions we make during our middle school and high school years could have more impact on when we die and how than the decisions we make at any other time in our lives? I didn't. But it's true. According to the Centers for Disease Control and Prevention (CDC), kids make more decisions in the teen years that impact mortality (when we die) and morbidity (the frequency of disease) than at any other time of life. Why? Because it's in the teen years that we develop our patterns of behavior. When we're teenagers, we begin making our first decisions – on our own, without adults standing nearby – about the lifestyle we will have.

If we smoke, we're more likely to get lung cancer and die early. If we drink alcohol, we're more likely to end up in substance abuse treatment. If we have unprotected sex, we're more likely to get an STD (sexually transmitted disease). If we eat tons of junk food and never exercise, we're more likely to be obese or have to deal with diabetes or heart disease.

I have learned all of this from working with my parents and writing this book. I'm the elder of two kids (I have a younger brother) and just graduated from high school. When I was six, my parents started a company that produces television documentaries and educational programs, for schools, about the life skills and character traits kids need to have the best chance at a successful, happy adult life. So – like it or not – I'm kind of the poster child for life's little lessons. Ever since I can remember, I was the test audience for the latest TV program or educational video on the life skill or character trait of the month. For most of high school, I felt like I got a double daily dose of all the information since I heard about it at home and sat through health classes and assemblies on the same subjects at school.

But I didn't know about the CDC statistic until my parents asked me to write this book. My parents and the producers, editors, educators, and researchers who have worked with them through the years have read a lot of data and interviewed hundreds of kids and parents about the pressures kids face and the choices they make, especially with when it comes to drugs, alcohol, sex, the Internet, bullying, and all the other things we hear about in school. I used to roll my eyes and moan when my mom would tell me another one of these stories, but to be honest, I was listening…and more than just a few stories made me think about things a little differently.

The summer after high school graduation, my parents asked if I would be interested in writing about some of the events that happened in my own life – some of the more difficult personal choices I had to make as a teen. They wanted to publish a book from a teenage perspective – something authentic, with an honest point of view. I didn't love the idea at first. My high school papers were the most sophisticated works I had ever written, and I certainly didn't make all As. Plus, I wasn't sure I wanted to put myself out there. Who could possibly want to read about my life anyway?

Then I read the CDC research. The choices we make as teens really do impact our lives – and deaths. That's not something to take lightly. But too often we do. I mean the great thing about being a teenager is being free to live in the here and now. It's the one time we get to feel invincible. But we're not.

I started thinking about some of the other reasons we make bad choices: stress, anxiety, the need to please, and all the tension in our day-to-day lives. Sometimes, I felt like I was living my life for someone else during high school. Rather than trying to figure out who I was, I was trying to be the person someone else wanted me to be. That needed to STOP too. I realized that if we could get kids and parents to think differently about the issues that confront teens, maybe it would help reduce the more dangerous choices we make. So I agreed to get involved.

We are all the sum total of our experiences – the stories and choices that change our lives. These are mostly mine, mixed in with some from other kids. All are written from my perspective. The names and places (and some of the details) have been changed to protect those involved. But every story is based on something that really happened to me or to someone else.

There's nothing earth-shattering. No secret revelations or formulas. Instead, this is a book about the real lives of teenagers and the day-to-day independent decisions we all have to make. I hope that I've said something here about being true to yourself and not conforming to what others want of you. And I hope it will help us all take our choices a little more seriously and realize that what we do today can change our lives tomorrow.

This may be bold but I think it's time for us to come together as a generation and stop the intense competition. Grades are important, going to a good college matters, material success is nice. But nothing means anything if we don't know who we are at our core. Because as I am learning...that's what success is: feeling comfortable about who we are, having values that we can hold on to in both good and bad times, and enjoying the things in life that matter most of all.

– Chandler DeWitt

Acknowledgments

My parents promised I wouldn't be working on this book alone – and I've learned the teamwork required in writing a book in and of itself builds character. Collin Siedor, an award-winning documentary producer and writer, coached me through the process and helped edit and write some of the stories. Psychologist and researcher, Dr. Gwen Schiada, lent her expertise to make sure the stories and messages would work in schools. Linda Bachmann, an extraordinary writer and editor, vetted copy and rewrote stories, questions, and activities up until the last minute. Emily Halevy, a news and documentary producer, reviewed the hours of video in the Connect with Kids library and came up stories that might fit when there wasn't a personal story to illustrate the issue. Ginger Schlanger, a writing coach and editor, helped me find my style. When all was in place, our book editor, Dr. Michelle Hutchinson, ensured consistency and clarity, reviewed every word, corrected run-on sentences and misspellings, and checked and rechecked grammar, punctuation, and style. My mom, Stacey DeWitt, pored over the stories making sure that we didn't exploit, misrepresent, offend, or hurt anyone in the process. Needless to say, this has been a group effort.

And finally, there were all the people in my life who helped shape my experiences – my teachers, coaches, counselors, friends, and family members whom I have been lucky enough to know during my childhood and teen years.

I

Inside Your Heart

Guy in the Glass

When you get what you want in your struggle for pelf,
And the world makes you King for a day,
Then go to the mirror and look at yourself,
And see what that guy has to say.
For it isn't your Father, or Mother, or Wife,
Who judgment upon you must pass.
The feller whose verdict counts most in your life
Is the guy staring back from the glass.

He's the feller to please, never mind all the rest,
For he's with you clear up to the end,
And you've passed your most dangerous, difficult test
If the guy in the glass is your friend.
You may be like Jack Horner and "chisel" a plum,
And think you're a wonderful guy,
But the man in the glass says you're only a bum
If you can't look him straight in the eye.
You can fool the whole world down the pathway of years,
And get pats on the back as you pass,
But your final reward will be heartaches and tears
If you've cheated the guy in the glass.

– Dale Wimbrow

Chapter 1

"Honesty and transparency make you vulnerable.
Be honest and transparent anyway."

– Mother Theresa

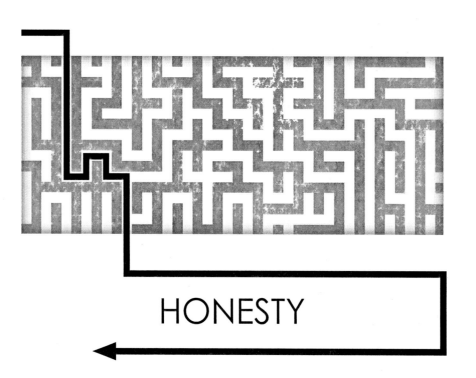

HONESTY

Game Over

Sometimes I think kids today face more pressures than any generation before ours. If you want to be successful at school, get into a good college, or get a scholarship to a good college, you have to make good grades, get involved in after-school activities, possibly take honors classes, make high scores on standardized tests, and volunteer for community service. It gets kind of crazy, feeling like you have to be good at everything – not just one or two things. And, once you get involved in all of these activities, it's hard to pull back or quit – even when you start to hate it.

I worry that all this focus on success is creating a kind of pressure that is unhealthy, especially when it comes to morals and character. Why? Because we're so busy that we do whatever it takes to get ahead. We take on the attitude that anything is okay if "the ends justify the means" and the end is...what? Success as defined by our classmates, our teachers, our school, our parents, but not by us.

I think we should stop, take a breath, and re-evaluate. I know I'm just a teenager, but I already get that life is short; we shouldn't waste our time trying to be the best at everything. Instead, we should try to get involved in things that excite us and mean something to us. Kids should not have to be part of everything in order to be successful. We should try lots of things and then focus on what really interests us. Our passion will lead us to success.

I learned this the hard way. I played competitive sports throughout elementary and middle school. Soccer and basketball were my primary sports. And to be competitive, I played year-round; during my schools' off-seasons, I played in a league called the AAU. By the end of middle school, basketball had become my focus, so when I started a new school in ninth grade, I did what I had always done – played basketball. I was a better-than-average guard, known as a good shooter – three pointers were my strength. Coaches liked that and my offensive play. But on defense, well, I had some weaknesses. Speed was not my best asset.

By the time I was a sophomore, my average day consisted of going to bed at one o'clock in the morning after studying and doing homework all night, and then getting up at five o'clock to go to basketball workouts. With only four hours of sleep behind me, I was already exhausted as I headed to my workouts (which we called agilities) before sunrise. I started saying to myself, "Why am I doing this?" That thought was kind of new for me. I had never questioned workouts before.

During 90 minutes of jump rope, sprints, squats, wall sits, hurdles, and more exercises to improve speed (already my weakness), the fastest girl on the team – who didn't really have to do any of this to beat everyone down the court – was next to me. Each day, when I walked into the gym, I began to realize that no matter how hard I tried or how hard she didn't, I'd never be as fast as she was. I was now in a bigger league in a big city and facing a whole new kind of competition. If this was about speed alone, she was going to win my spot.

No matter how hot or cold it was outside, I would feel perspiration running down my legs, leaving puddles when I sat on the gym floor.

After the workouts were over, I was like a zombie, but I still had seven hours of school ahead of me. Throughout the day, I couldn't keep my head up in class. I missed important notes, my body ached, and worst of all, I couldn't get my coach's voice out of my mind. I kept hearing, "You are too slow!" In my head, I answered back, "So what! I don't care!"

On one particular day, when I had to take a history test after lunch, I was so tired that I couldn't concentrate. The questions didn't make sense. I was so ready to be done that I made up answers that at least sounded reasonable. At the end, I knew I had done poorly on my exam and it would hurt my grade in the course – just one more thing to worry about.

Between classes, I was walking with a friend who was telling me about some problem she had with her boyfriend or her mom or something, but I was so tired I couldn't even focus. I knew she could tell that I wasn't really paying attention to her, but I couldn't help it. Since friends mean everything to me, it killed me that I wasn't there for her. I was in my own little world, too worried about sports and grades and friends and a hundred other things, and too tired to think about it all.

Finally the day was over, but only the school day. I still had a two-hour AAU basketball practice.

At practice, we started with stretching and more running. Sure enough, my coach ran over and laid it on me. "You're too slow! You gotta be quicker!" This from a guy who was forty-five pounds overweight and couldn't run a mile to save his life. I tried to muster all the energy I had left, but I didn't really get any faster. The ridicule continued, and although I was boiling with rage inside, I stayed and took his taunts. I didn't walk out the door or say, "So what! I don't care!" All I did was apologize and say I would get better

Then we went into drills: three-man weave and shooting practice. The coach said he didn't approve of our level of play, so he made us do a running drill. Each person on the team had to shoot two free throws; if someone missed, we had to run a sprint. I think we ran nineteen sprints in that practice – and that's before the running we had to do at the end of the session.

When it was time to scrimmage, I completely froze. I dreaded this part, knowing I would be the one to mess up. Plus, the girls around me were sweating more than I could drink. For two hours, a dozen slimy, sweating girls bumped up against each other. When I was little I didn't think about it. Now, something had changed. To me, it seemed disgusting.

Once we started playing, I was nervous. My hands were dripping wet and, of course, I messed up and turned the ball over. The other team scored off my mistake. The coach chewed me out in front of everyone. And, once again, I wondered, "Why am I here? What good is this doing me?"

I knew in my heart that if I continued to play on this team, my self-confidence would be gone by the end of the season. I sat on the bench during games praying that I wouldn't have to go in; my nerves took over my body. I felt sick to my stomach and broke out in a sweat. If the coach called my name to go in, I started to shake all over. I desperately wanted to tough it out, but I didn't know that I could.

For me, hanging in there when you feel like quitting requires believing in what you're doing. To put up with the yelling and the pain and the hardship, it had to mean something… to me. But, at that point, basketball had lost its meaning.

After practice was over, I went home to face three hours of homework: writing a paper, doing forty-five math problems, completing four Spanish workbook pages, and studying for a biology quiz. It was a long list because the night before I had fallen asleep after practice, and now the homework was starting to stack up. I knew I wouldn't get to bed until after midnight. And the next day, I was supposed to wake up and do it all over again. Thanks, but no thanks. I decided that I was done.

The hardest part came next. I had to tell my parents I wanted to quit basketball. I had been playing for seven years, and they had invested a lot of time and money in it. I didn't want to do it anymore. I was miserable, and I had to figure out a way to convince them that quitting was the right thing to do.

That night, after dinner, I started talking to my mom and dancing around the subject. I finally just told her: I want to quit basketball. She called my dad in to talk with both of us. I was nervous. I explained that I had completely lost my love for the game. It was no fun anymore. My desire was gone.

At first my parents weren't happy; in simple terms they told me to suck it up. They said I had an obligation. They wanted me to be loyal to the school, my coaches, and my teammates. I tried to explain that I needed to be loyal to myself first – before I tried to please others.

They were quiet then. They started to really hear me. I told them that I felt like a constant disappointment when I was playing basketball. When I was younger, I had felt confident on the court, but now the game was drowning me. No matter how many people might be upset, I had to do this for myself. Then my dad said, "If this is how it makes you feel and you don't love the game anymore, there's no sense in playing."

I breathed a sigh of relief; I think they understood that while I loved recreational sports as a kid, I did not have the passion for the level of competition involved in high school. There were just too many other things I wanted to do. I had friends who still loved the game and were driven to go through the agilities and the extra practices. They thrived on the "thrill of victory," which was great for them but not me. So, as hard as it was, I was honest with my parents. Even though it took a while, they accepted what I wanted and supported me and my decision. I slept better that night than I had in weeks.

Next I worked up the courage to tell my coaches of my decision to quit. I met with each and finally got the words out: that I just could not find the drive to do what they and my teammates deserved. Believe it or not, all went better than expected. No yelling. No scenes. Each listened and reacted respectfully and thoughtfully. My high school coach, who saw me every day in the hallways, really cared about me as person, not just a player and was very understanding.

Every day I am so glad that I made the decision to quit. I have never looked back. Regardless of the reactions from other people, I still believe you have to stand up for yourself. No one else is going to do that for you.

What came next? I had heard a lot about my school's community service and peer leadership programs. In the back of my mind I always thought I'd like to get involved. After thinking it over for a few months, I applied to be a school peer leader. That was halfway through my sophomore year – and a big change for me. People who thought they knew me – and knew me only as an athlete – were seeing something new.

> "Regardless of the reactions from other people, I still believe you have to stand up for yourself. No one else is going to do that for you."

Peer leaders helped new students adjust to school. We showed them the ropes and gave them the opportunity to meet new people. I liked doing this; it felt natural to me. Later, I became a retreat leader, as well. I learned to play the guitar and joined the chorus – things I could do because I had the time to spend on the activities I really enjoyed much more than competitive sports. It all started because I followed my instincts and tried out for something that seemed genuinely interesting to me, not because I was working hard at playing politics and trying to compete with other kids. I didn't feel pressure to rise through the ranks. I don't think I even realized it at first, but these leadership positions helped me rebuild my confidence. Little by little, that feeling of being worthless was fading away; I felt that I had a purpose.

As a retreat leader and peer leader, I could hardly wait for our weekly meetings. Though it was a lot of work, to me it was fun and meaningful, just like competitive athletics may be fun and meaningful for someone else.

I also learned that my coaches, my teachers, and my parents didn't want me to be involved in something that didn't mean anything to me. I thought I was performing for them. They thought I liked what I was doing. And by being honest, I cleared the air and no one was disappointed.

I accomplished more for myself in three months of service work and peer leadership than I did in two years of high school basketball. I didn't do it to build my résumé or impress my parents or win awards. This work honored who I was, not what somebody else wanted me to be. I think rewards come if you find something that fits you, that you're good at, that you want to do. And I don't think you can leave those choices up to someone else. Game over.

Discussion/Self-Reflection Questions

1. In the chapter, Chandler says, "Kids face more pressures than any generation before ours." Do you agree with this statement? Why or why not?

2. Do you believe young people can have a mid-life crisis in high school? Explain.

3. The chapter begins with this quote from Mother Theresa: "Honesty and transparency make you vulnerable. Be honest and transparent anyway." What does it mean to be vulnerable? Is it sometimes hard to be honest?

4. What type of pressures do you feel in your own life? What are some ways that you can deal with stress in a healthy way?

5. Chandler talks about finding her passion. What are you passionate about; what excites you and means something to you?

6. What does it mean to be honest with yourself? Why is this important?

7. Chandler talks about her peer leadership and service program involvement and shares that it just felt right to her. What tells you that something is right for you? How do you know?

8. Do you agree with Chandler that it's okay to quit something if you're unhappy or doing it for the wrong reasons? Explain. Have you had this situation in your own life? How did you deal with it? Are there things you wish you would have done differently? Explain.

9. Chandler believes that our morals and character are in danger and says that oftentimes students take on the attitude that anything is okay if "the end justifies the means." Do you believe that anything is okay if "the end justifies the means?" Explain. Where do you draw the line? What are some ways you can keep from crossing the line?

10. Chandler shares that it's important to please yourself before pleasing others and to be loyal to yourself first. What does this mean? What do you think about that statement? What are some things you can do to make sure that you are being loyal to yourself? What is your "checklist" for knowing that you are being loyal to who you are?

Journaling Activity

After reading the story related to the character trait of honesty, define the trait in your own words in the space below:

What key messages or lessons did you take away from the story about honesty?

The story infers that being honest with one's strengths, weaknesses, and desires leads to success. What is your personal definition of success? Are you living up to your definition? Explain.

Chandler writes that she "slept better that night than I had in weeks" when she finally told her parents of her decision to quit basketball and be honest with herself. What helps you or would help you sleep better at night?

Chapter 2

"Our greatest strength lies not in never failing, but in rising each time we fall."

– Ralph Waldo Emerson

PERSEVERANCE

A Matter of Degree

Juan was a soft-spoken, quiet kid who ran the 440 on the varsity track team and was the starting middle linebacker on the football team at his high school. He was one of the people interviewed for a documentary on smart kids that don't do well in school. And I have to say that now, every time I think I can't do something or want to give up, I think about Juan.

I saw Juan's story as I was logging video tapes as part of my summer job at my parent's company. It was the part of the job I hated the most. Usually, I could barely keep my eyes open. I had to pop the tape into the video deck and set what's called a time code. Then, I had to type every word that was spoken on the tape and make sure that I included a time code for every paragraph as well. On one particular morning, all I could think about was going through the motions and getting off work so I could meet some friends that afternoon. I was tired from the night before and my parents were watching me pretty closely, saying that I was staying up too late in the summer when I had to be at work early the next day. So I walked back to the edit room, turned on the video deck, and picked up the first tape on the stack; a young guy named Juan was face-to-face with the camera.

He told the interviewer that he wasn't a particularly good student. In fact, he had flunked most of his classes his freshman year and had to start all over again. At that point, the guidance counselor had told him that he ought to get off the college prep track—that it was too challenging for him—and that he should switch to the career tech or vocational track. In his school, he said your academic track was based on whether your guidance counselor thought you could handle the workload. If the guidance counselor thought you could handle the workload, then you were put in the college prep track, which meant you would probably go to college. Those kids would take advanced math, small group seminars in English lit, and lots of advanced placement or honors classes. But, if your grades were not so good and the guidance counselor thought you were not smart enough to handle the classes, you were put in the so-called general courses that were easier and included classes like drafting, graphic design, and bookkeeping.

As you can guess, no one thought Juan was college material. They just assumed Juan didn't have the brains to make good grades and never bothered to ask why he had failed his freshman classes. So, at the end of ninth grade, Juan's guidance counselor told him to get off the college prep track, that those classes were just too difficult. The counselor told Juan to switch to the general classes and that way he might do a little better, might improve his grades or at least not flunk anything. And Juan said, "No." It was a turning point.

Juan had decided he was going to college. There was no other option. He didn't care what the guidance counselor thought. That was his plan and there was no changing it. I think his decision was amazing in some ways.

First of all, for him to look the guidance counselor in the face and say, "Nope, I'm not doing that. I want to stay on the college prep track because I want to go to college," took a lot of nerve. He was 14 years old. He was a kid telling an adult that she was wrong, that he was going to fight against the recommendation, and that he was smart enough to handle the tougher workload.

That's the other thing. Imagine a counselor, an adult, saying to you "Hey, you're not very smart, so just take the easy way out." That would feel pretty bad but would also be pretty tempting, especially for someone who had just flunked his freshman year.

But even though he had failed the year before, something inside of Juan made him believe in himself. Even though he wasn't sure why he had failed, he was convinced that he could figure it out and could go to college. So, Juan pleaded with the guidance counselor and convinced her to let Juan stay on college prep track and retake the courses he had failed.

In tenth grade, Juan took ninth-grade language arts again and discovered his problem. His teacher was kind of a bitter, tough, old lady who few people liked. She had a reputation for being terrible and had been at the school since the beginning of time. One day, she asked Juan to stay after class. When he walked up to her desk, she said "Juan, you can pass this class. I know you can. But, first, we have to teach you to read."

Juan was shocked. He knew how to read. He had been reading for school all of his life. But what the teacher explained is that he couldn't read well enough. When Juan read something, he would almost immediately forget it. He was spending so much energy on reading the words that he never really understood the sentences. But his teacher, Mrs. Walsh, would change all that. When she had him read out loud or write a couple of paragraphs about the previous nights' literature assignment, it didn't take her long to figure out that he had a reading problem. And she was tough. I mean determined. It bugged her having a kid who couldn't read sitting in front of her language arts class. She and Juan both were very determined to fix that.

> "Juan was shocked. He knew how to read. He had been reading for school all of his life. But what the teacher explained is that he couldn't read well enough."

So, every Monday, Wednesday, and Friday, Mrs. Walsh made Juan stay after class, even if that meant he'd be late for lunch or miss it. (I bet she missed as many lunches as he did.) She would drill him on grammar and sentence structure and vocabulary, and they would read and talk and read and talk and then read some more. Every other day for a year, whatever it took, she was going to teach him to read.

And it worked. It wasn't easy, he said, but in tenth grade, Juan passed all his classes. No As...but all Bs and Cs. It was a start. He said it was amazing how much easier those language arts and history and social studies classes were...if you could read.

He played football in the fall, ran track in the spring, and went to classes all year long. He was well-liked, had some close friends, a girlfriend, and worked hard to pass his classes. After ninth grade, he never got a grade lower than a C.

In the first semester of his senior year, it was time to apply to college. Most of the college prep kids had visited a bunch of schools over the summer; they had talked with their parents and the college counselor about what colleges to apply to and why, and most were busy filling out applications and writing essays and getting teacher recommendations. But it wasn't so easy for Juan. His grade point average wasn't that great, and he wasn't ranked very high in the class. His transcript would show that it took him five years rather than four to get through high school because he failed so many classes his freshman year.

He walked in to the college guidance office, and the counselor said he wasn't sure about Juan going to college. "Juan," he said," let's shoot high and try to get you into a two-year program."

"A two-year college?" Juan asked.

"Yeah," the counselor answered. "Like a community college...we have several of them in town, and they're not hard to get into. Some aren't all that challenging. It would be a good fit for you."

Juan said he thought for a moment before he responded, but then he said, "I'd like to go to a full, four-year school...a college that's fully accredited, where I can get a degree, a four-year degree."

But the counselor didn't agree. "I don't think so," he said. "I think the best you can do is community college right here at home and if that goes well...I mean...listen, if you get really good grades, maybe one day you can transfer to one of the state schools."

They talked for a few more minutes, and then Juan walked out of the college guidance office and never walked in there again. He had made up his mind. He was going to a four-year university. He had decided.

So, Juan started looking for colleges that might take a chance on him—small, four-year schools that were not well known, that might like an athletic kid whose grades were bad at first but who had showed steady improvement—especially if he could get a recommendation from his language arts teacher. He searched. He printed applications, filled them out, and sent them in.

One school answered. It was a four-year, private college, fully accredited. But their acceptance was conditional. He would have to go to summer school and prove himself first. He would have to take a full load of summer classes and get no lower than a B. And so, that's exactly what he did.

Four years later, he finished college with a bachelor's degree. By the end of his sophomore year, he had made the dean's list and continued to make it every semester until he graduated. Today, no one calls him Juan. They call him Doctor Juan because of his Ph.D.

Discussion/Self-Reflection Questions

1. The chapter opens with this quote from Ralph Waldo Emerson, "Our greatest strength lies not in never failing, but in rising each time we fall." What does this mean to you?

2. What does perseverance mean? How important is this character trait to you?

3. Who shows perseverance in this story besides Juan?

4. Why do you think it was so important for Juan to persevere and not give up on his dream of going to a four-year college?

5. Has anyone ever tried to convince you that you couldn't accomplish a goal that was important to you? What happened?

6. What might have happened if Juan had listened to the people who had encouraged him to give up?

7. Can you describe a situation in which you have demonstrated perseverance? Explain.

8. Describe a situation in which you did not succeed. What did you learn from that experience? Did it change your outlook or influence your future?

9. What is a Ph.D.? What does it take to get a Ph.D.?

10. How do you think Juan went from flunking ninth grade to getting a Ph.D.?

11. Are there people in your life who support your dreams and goals? How can they help you achieve them?

Journaling Activity

The chapter begins with a quote from Ralph Waldo Emerson. Emerson, who lived from 1803-1882, was an American philosopher and poet, and known as a champion of individualism. What does individualism mean? How do you see that movement reflected in 21st-century society?

Chandler related to perseverance by watching a video segment about Juan's experiences. Describe a situation in which you have learned something from someone else's experience.

Write a letter to yourself. Remind yourself of your good qualities and your goals, and offer encouragement to continue the hard work and perseverance you'll need to succeed.

Let's say that Dr. Juan becomes your first college professor. Write what you think his words of encouragement might be to his new students during his first lecture.

Albert Einstein said, "It's not that I'm so smart, it's just that I stay with problems longer." What happens when you stay with problems longer? What distracts you? How do you deal with those distractions?

Chapter 3

"The greatest way to live with honor in this world is to be what we pretend to be."

– Socrates

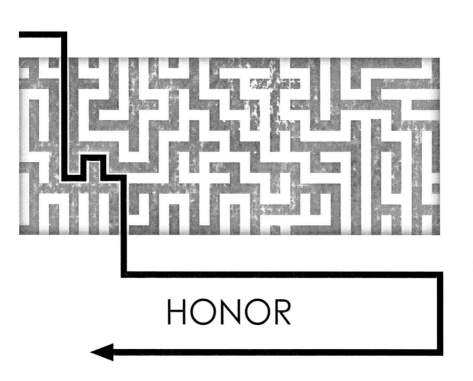

HONOR

Truth or Fraud

I've never been extremely focused on academics. My grades weren't awful in high school but not quite good enough to please my parents or make the honor roll. I'd say I was an average student – not one of the brilliant kids but not at the bottom of the pile either. Bottom line: I preferred to do almost anything other than study, even though grades seemed to be the one thing that defined how smart you are, what colleges accept you, or whether you're lazy or hard-working. I wasn't sure if it was about winning the approval of the teacher or making my parents happy, because I didn't care too much whether I had an A or a C in a class, but I pretended I cared. I acted like I was trying hard and doing the best I could. And, until my junior year, I always wondered why my grades meant so much to everybody else but so little to me.

I went to a high school where most people made good grades. Your report card, class rank, and overall grade point average were kind of a badge of honor. And I played the game: I acted like the classes were really tough, and I stood around with the others kids before homeroom complaining about how late we had stayed up studying the night before, how busy we were, and how tired we were from all the homework. My light would shine under my bedroom door until one or two in the morning most nights, and my parents would think I was killing myself studying when really, I was checking out Facebook or i-chatting with a friend. It wasn't that I didn't study at all. I did – just enough to get by. Usually, I'd coast along in the first part of the semester and tell my parents, who asked almost daily, that things were going great. I would show up, participate in class, and make pretty good grades on the first couple of quizzes. Then, I'd fail one quiz or two, rebound on the test, fail another pop quiz because I blew off the reading assignment for homework, and rally again for the second test. All resulting in a kind of yo-yo approach to school that usually landed me with a couple of A's mostly B's and a C or two on the first progress report.

My parents worried – was school just too tough for me? They would sit me down, and we would talk it through. I would tell them I was really trying, and soon I started to believe it myself. My grades always hovered at mostly B's and sometimes a C.

Then, in my junior year, I took chemistry and hit an all time low. I hated science and could have cared less about chemistry. My pattern had worked well before but not in this class. I couldn't rally like I usually did. When progress reports rolled around, I had a D, not a C or a B. I knew I couldn't fake my way through a D or an F, and my parents were threatening much more than a heart-to-heart talk. They were now checking every paper and insisting that I bring everything home. My mom was like a nervous cat pacing around me constantly and asking whether I needed a tutor. And then I bombed the test I actually had to pass to have any chance of keeping a B in the class. I remember getting it back – a big 64 circled in red Sharpie. That score was a D in my school. That meant I was close to failing and about to be exposed.

I went home that afternoon and my mom popped the question as soon as I walked through the door. "Did you get your chemistry test back?" I had been dreading this moment all day trying to figure out how I was going to handle it. I could picture that disappointed look on my mother's face that I had come to know so well. And so – it was here – the moment of truth. Then I made a decision. I lied. I looked her right in the eye and said, "We didn't get the test back – still not sure what I made." I knew I was just postponing what had to happen sooner or later. I didn't care. I was tired and didn't want to deal with all the conflict. I told myself it wasn't a big lie. I guess I was hoping that she wouldn't find out until I took another chem test. I thought if I could do a lot better on the second test, maybe that 64 wouldn't look so bad…at least I could say I was improving.

I worried about the lie for a second or two but then decided to move on. No big deal; I'd just tell her my teacher hadn't given us our grade for the next week or so until at least my quiz grades had improved.

After dinner, I went up to my room, flipped on my light, and logged on to Facebook. I needed a distraction, a break.

At about the same time I logged on to my computer, my mom logged on to hers – but not to chat. She decided to check out my school's website where teachers can post your grades. Unfortunately, when I had lied to my mom, I hadn't thought about my teacher or mother racing to the online website the minute we got the chemistry test back.

My mom signed on to the site, entered her password, and there it was

– evidence that I had gotten the test back that day. She yelled for me to come downstairs but didn't sound mad. I thought she just wanted me to help fold the laundry. Then I saw the look on her face. It wasn't anger but disappointment. And the long, long talk began. It was the kind that lasts an hour, and you can't leave, and you can't roll your eyes, and you can't say anything back. You just have to listen and nod your head and promise you'll do better next time and that you will never lie again. And, I know it may not sound like it, but I meant it. Lying and disappointing my parents were not near the top of my list of things I liked to do. But it was more than that. I realized I had not only lied to them, but that I had been lying to myself.

I actually was disappointed about the chemistry test grade. I didn't want to get a D in a class or even a C if I could help it. I wanted people to think I was smart, wanted my parents to be proud of me, wanted to be an interesting person, and even wanted to learn about things that interested me, like music, and art history, and writing – not so much chemistry, but I didn't want to fail it. But the bottom line was that at the time I wasn't willing to do the work or to give up other stuff like Facebook or my favorite TV show or the phone to do what it took – real studying – to become the person I was pretending to be. I had hit a new kind of low – lying to keep up the pretense.

"...at the time I wasn't willing to do the work or to give up other stuff like Facebook or my favorite TV show or the phone to do what it took – real studying – to become the person I was pretending to be. I had hit a new kind of low – lying to keep up the pretense."

You might think it ended there, that I just decided I would be a little more disciplined and start studying harder, and that all of a sudden my grades would improve. And some of that did happen. I pulled my chemistry grade up by the end of the semester, but something I didn't expect happened too.

That night, as my mom rambled on, I started thinking about what was important to me. My parents were always urging me to get good grades, to do my best – even though on any given day I wasn't completely sure what that was – so I could get into a really "good" college – and I wasn't exactly sure what that was either. But as I started thinking about what was meaningful to me, I realized that while everyone seemed to be competing to get into the "best" schools, I wanted to go to a school that offered more than just strong academics. And, I didn't want to spend all of my time with my head in a book. I wanted to meet new people, travel, play intramural sports, and have a full college experience. I liked to learn, but I was more of a practical, hands-on person who liked to learn through experience and doing things. I was social, athletic, creative, but not extremely academic.

So when my mom took a breath, I said, "You know, I shouldn't have lied. And, I have been lying about more than just this test. I shouldn't pretend I'm studying when I'm not. And I should work harder to actually make the grades that I want to make. I promise I'm going to make more effort from now on. But, I also think my grades should reflect my effort. And, if I don't make the grades I need to get into the college I want to go to or that we can afford, then I'll suffer the consequences. So, I really think everyone needs to calm down and back off a little bit. I don't want to go to a college where all I can do is study to make it through."

There – it was out. And I wasn't even sure I knew that until then. What I did know was that I didn't want to lie anymore or pretend that I was someone I wasn't, not for my friends, my teachers, or my parents.

That night my parents and I came to an understanding. I needed to maintain as close to a B average as possible, and in classes like chemistry or other subjects that were very difficult I would do the best I could on any given day. If I slacked off, I alone would pay the price. No more lectures or nagging from my parents. It was up to me. After that, I actually made slightly better grades. I stopped acting like I was studying so hard and so busy all the time when I wasn't. I stopped worrying whether people thought I was smart. I got into the college that I wanted to attend. I am on my way – and free because now I am who I pretend to be.

Discussion/Self-Reflection Questions

1. How do you define honor? How important is honor as a character trait?

2. What other character traits do you think impact honor? Explain.

3. What was Chandler pretending to be? What did she do in order to pretend?

4. Chandler describes lying to her mom about her chemistry test grade and then realizing "I had not only lied to them, but I had been lying to myself." Can you think of a time that you lied to someone? What was the outcome? How did it make you feel?

5. Chandler writes that her parents were always urging her to get good grades and do her best – even though, on any given day, she wasn't completely sure what that was. What does doing your best mean to you? Can you really do your best every day?

6. What are some of your long-term goals? What do you need to do know in order to achieve those goals? What obstacles do you face? Who do you look to for help?

7. Chandler talks about the honor roll at her school. What does it take to get on the honor roll at your school? As we talk about honor, what else might an honor roll recognize besides grades?

8. If you are able to honor yourself and others, how will that benefit you? How will that benefit those around you?

9. The chapter begins with this quote from Socrates, "The greatest way to live with honor in this world is to be what we pretend to be." What does this quote mean to you? What are some of the things you pretend to be?

10. Socrates was a classical Greek philosopher who lived from 469 BC to 399 BC. Despite the vast changes in our society over the centuries, what do you think are some of the human challenges that remain unchanged? What advances, like technology, make those challenges even greater?

Journaling Activity

Chandler did not want to face her parents with the results of her test grade. If this happened to you, what would you do? Describe the likely outcome.

This story relating to the character trait of honor explores being truthful to oneself and to others. There are other interpretations of honor. Describe honor in your own words in the space below.

The Medal of Honor is the highest military decoration awarded by the United States government. Research the story of one of the award recipients. How did this individual demonstrate honor and other character traits?

Take a look at this week's news – online, in print, or on TV. Can you find a recent story in which honor played a role?

This section of the book begins with "Guy in the Glass" by Dale Wimbrow. How does this poem relate to honor?

Chapter 4

"What convinces is conviction."

– Lyndon B. Johnson

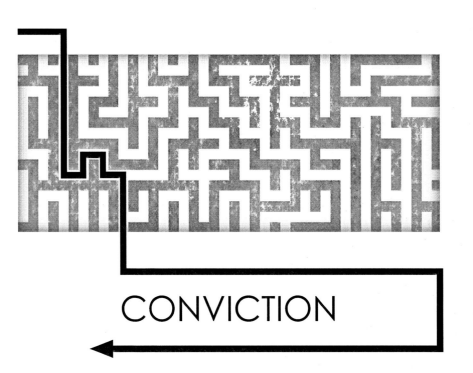

CONVICTION

The Art of Passion

Dr. Jake Foreman was a man for all generations. He was 52 years old when I had him as a teacher during my senior year in high school, but he could have easily been 25. To his students, he was one of the coolest and most well-respected teachers in the school. We related to him and, to a large degree, were in awe of him. I think it was because of his convictions and passion – qualities that, he taught me, transcend time.

Dr. Foreman taught Advanced Placement Art History, an elective I took even though I didn't know much about Art History and didn't have a special interest in it. What I did know was the reputation of Dr. Foreman and the class. Everybody wanted to take it. There was a waiting list to get in. So I was one of the first to sign-up. After the first few days of class, I began to get a clue as to why the course was so popular.

Dr. Foreman didn't look particularly artsy. He wore black or gray pants, black leather shoes, and glasses. But, he also rode a motorcycle, lived in a house modeled after Frank Lloyd Wright's designs, and everyday wore a '60s throw-back tie clip to school – not traditional by any means.

When he spoke about his subject, his expression and passion lit up the room. I remember realizing the impact the course was going to have on me when we began studying Hellenistic art, a Greek form that is intensely dramatic and that ended up fascinating me. But, it was when we were studying Vincent Van Gogh that I finally understood the role Dr. Foreman played in my newfound interest. Foreman's views on Van Gogh would ultimately convince me that art history could tell us something about ourselves.

I had been excited about studying Van Gogh since the beginning of the course, because he was the one artist I knew something about. He was the guy who cut off his ear. Van Gogh was a madman who also suffered from epilepsy and had a pretty unhappy life working as an art dealer and bookstore clerk before ending up in an insane asylum. I didn't really understand why he was so revered, particularly since he was half-crazed, but when Foreman explained concepts, I began to appreciate art and Van Gogh on a whole new level. Each day we would come to class, and Foreman would turn off the lights and turn on the LCD projector. You could hear the low hum of projector as our teacher clicked through the slides of Van Gogh's works. Dr. Foreman would click one slide, walk to the back of the room, and talk in a slow, steady rhythm that sounded more like a poetry reading than a lecture. Art History wasn't a fast-paced class that flew by, but somehow, my teacher's movement and tone created a slow energy that spread across the room. He had an intense charisma that made you want to listen and learn.

Foreman taught me that to really understand an artist, you have to focus on his work in the context of what people wrote about him and how his community viewed him. That information added to the mystery of Van Gogh. I began to sense a beauty and special quality to his paintings. Starry Night, Starry Night over the Rhone, and Night Café were and are still my three favorites. Van Gogh did not become famous until after he died, and no one thought he had any talent when he was alive. He had no money and no family members who believed in him except his brother Theodore. Vincent Van Gogh lived a depressing and lonely day-to-day existence, but his paintings showed something else. He had thick brushstrokes and used rich, thick paint on the canvas. He also used vibrant colors but no defining lines, so when viewing his works, your eyes stay in constant motion and never fixate on one particular point. Foreman helped me realize that while Van Gogh was half-crazed and tormented throughout most of his life, there was a part of him that was untouched by all that; he was able to create some of the most beautiful and intriguing pieces of art in our history. Somehow, his talent was protected even though his life was a mess.

> "Art History wasn't a fast-paced class that flew by, but somehow, my teacher's movement and tone created a slow energy that spread across the room. He had an intense charisma that made you want to listen and learn."

Dr. Foreman became a legend at our school and word spread. Soon, he developed a reputation throughout our city and was interviewed for a local teacher spotlight story on the news. On TV, he talked about his philosophy of teaching. He said he wanted students to be able to connect to the subject he was teaching to their own lives. And, that he hoped he could teach students to reserve judgments about people and ideas and instead ask questions.

It was Dr. Foreman's principles of teaching and dedication to art that pushed me to ask questions. He convinced me to look a little deeper and find the beauty in life. And, that being true to your own convictions and passions is contagious.

Discussion/Self-Reflection Questions

1. What does conviction mean to you? How important is conviction as a character trait?

2. Chandler writes that it was Dr. Foreman's principles of teaching and dedication to art that pushed her to ask questions. Who in your life demonstrates this kind of conviction? In what way(s)? How does that influence you?

3. What would you say is your passion at this point in your life? How might that change as you get older?

4. Has there been a situation in your own life in which you demonstrated conviction? Explain.

5. Have your convictions ever changed someone else's behavior? Explain.

6. Chandler writes of the influence her art history teacher had on her outlook, perhaps beyond just the subject at hand. Is there a teacher you have had that has influenced your outlook or character development – beyond the subject he or she was teaching? In what way?

7. What do you believe is the difference between having strong convictions and strong opinions?

8. The chapter begins with this quote from Lyndon B. Johnson: What convinces is conviction. What do think this means?

9. Who was Lyndon B. Johnson? How do you think his experiences defined his conviction?

10. What other character traits require conviction? In order to have conviction, what other character traits might one possess?

Journaling Activity

Look in a dictionary and identify the different definitions of conviction. How do you think those definitions are similar? How do you think they are different?

The chapter describes the influence of a teacher, beyond the subject matter at hand. Write a letter thanking one of your teachers for his or her efforts – and influence.

Think about conviction and peer pressure. Do you think there is any correlation? Explain.

Choose a public leader in the media spotlight today. Describe his or her conviction on a particular topic. How does he or she go about influencing public opinion?

This section of the book begins with the Dale Wimbrow poem "Guy in the Glass." How do you think it relates to the character trait of conviction?

Chapter 5

"Integrity is what we do, what we say,
and what we say we do."

– Don Galer

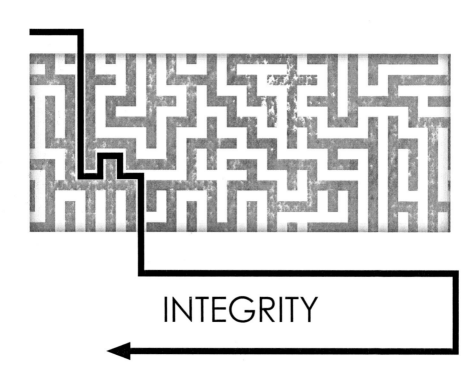

INTEGRITY

The Great Fake

It was 2:30 on a Thursday afternoon, and everybody was sick of history. If you looked around the room, you could see people sneaking text messages while hiding their phones in the zipper pockets of their backpacks. The bell was about to ring – class was almost over. Then, the teacher walked to the whiteboard and put up the homework assignment: Paper due tomorrow. *Are you kidding me?* I thought. I knew I was not alone. I could hear everyone groaning just softly enough not to get in trouble. The paper was supposed to be about the 9/11 attacks on the World Trade Center. The teacher said it should be an easy topic. We had been talking about it for two days in class, and there was plenty of information on the Internet. I still don't know why the teacher assigned a last-minute paper, giving us only one day to work on it, but he did, and nobody was happy about it, particularly my friend Kurt.

Kurt was an overscheduled overachiever. Sometimes I got tired just talking to him. He played football and soccer, was on the student council, and was involved in a ton of other activities. While most of my classmates hung out in the parking lot after class each day, Kurt ran around the school checking off his list of things to do.

In history class that day, he was overwhelmed. His desk was behind mine, so we walked out together. "D— — n it," was the first thing he said to me. "Why did he have to give us this paper tonight? There is no way I can get it done. I've got…" and he rambled off a list of stuff. I felt a little sorry for him but wasn't really paying much attention. Kurt was always busy. I had my own worries about getting the paper done too.

The next day, Kurt came into history class smiling and talking. When it came time to turn our papers in, he passed it up the row, and I glanced down. It looked just like Kurt – perfect. Mine, on the other hand, had a smudge on the front page and a typo that I had missed the night before. *Oh well*, I thought, *I have a B in the class now. One typo won't kill me.*

I forgot about the paper until the following week when we got them back. I got my standard B. Kurt? An A, naturally. And, our teacher announced that he planned to put the best paper in the school's monthly literary magazine, which published poetry, short stories, and essays written by students. Whose paper got that honor? Kurt's.

I remembered how much complaining Kurt had done the day we got the project and wondered how he had now pulled off the best paper in the class. Was he brilliant? Did he work like a dog and get no sleep? Or was his talk about how busy he was all the time just that: talk? I wasn't sure, but here he was, getting the A and having his work published in the school magazine. And there was more.

The next week, Kurt's paper showed up in our local newspaper. There was a feature story about a local kid who had written an emotional essay about 9/11. At school, he was praised on the website and during the morning announcements. "Everyone should stop by and pick up the local newspaper to read the article," the announcer said over the intercom. Kurt was on a roll. Everything was working in his favor. And then…he cracked.

The next time I logged onto the school's website to check homework, I noticed Kurt's paper was no longer posted. Hmm…it was unusual for teachers to take things like that down so quickly, but in English class, one of Kurt's best friends told me why the paper had been removed. It turned out that Kurt wasn't quite the perfect student everyone thought he was. He had gone to our history teacher and admitted that he hadn't written the entire paper. Some of it was his, but he had gotten some of it off the Internet. For the next two days, it was all anybody could talk about when Kurt wasn't around. Everyone kept asking, "Why did he turn himself in? Nobody would have ever known. He should have just kept the A and moved on."

But I think Kurt had been cheating just a little bit for long time. My bet is that he stole a line or two from the Internet pretty regularly, copied homework from friends when he was overwhelmed from all his other activities, and maybe even took advantage of answers someone gave him for a test or two. Several kids I knew did it – a little, not a lot. And sort of like a white lie, most told themselves it was no big deal, especially if you didn't get caught. I mean who did it really hurt?

"When everyone is making a fuss over you, it's harder to ignore that voice inside your head that hounds you when you do something wrong."

But when Kurt started getting all that extra attention – all the congratulations and praise – that probably changed things. When everyone is making a fuss over you, it's harder to ignore that voice inside your head that hounds you when you do something wrong. It's harder to forget what you've done and move on because everybody keeps reminding you what a great thing you did that you really didn't do. So, Kurt told the truth – probably to ease his guilt. I've felt like that before. Sometimes it seems like any punishment is better than living every day in the spotlight when you feel like a fake.

Kurt had to apologize in writing, had to give a talk about plagiarism to a bunch of freshmen, and probably was assigned a bunch of extra work by our history teacher. I never asked him about it. I just kept talking to him as if nothing had happened.

I liked Kurt much better after that. He didn't seem so perfect, so distant, and that made him more likeable. And, I really respected him for telling the truth. Kurt did have integrity after all. He had forgotten about it for a while, but it never really left him. And, in my mind, he probably got it back for good when he decided to come clean.

Discussion/Self-Reflection Questions

1. Chandler writes that cheating is somewhat common. Do you agree with her? Why/ Why not?

2. Why do you think people cheat? What is your opinion of people who cheat? Explain.

3. Students today have been called "The Internet Generation." Do you think today's technology makes cheating easier? In what ways can technology impact one's integrity? Explain.

4. What does it mean to have integrity? How do you define it?

5. The chapter begins with the quote: Integrity is what we do, what we say, and what we say we do. What does this mean to you?

6. Has there been a situation in your own life in which you compromised your integrity to get what you wanted? Explain. Do you wish you would have done something differently?

7. Has there been a situation in your own life where you were tempted to compromise your integrity but you didn't? Explain. How did it feel to keep your integrity?

8. What are some ways that we can be strong and not compromise our integrity when we are tempted?

9. Have you ever encountered a situation in which you did have integrity when it could have been easier not to? Explain. How did it feel to do the right thing?

10. What are the consequences of not showing integrity? How can it impact your relationships?

Journaling Activity

After reading the story related to the character trait of integrity, define the trait in your own words.

Think about recent news stories involving business, politics, sports, or celebrities. Describe situations in which integrity was involved. Do you think integrity is valued by society today?

If a friend offered you a copy of next week's test he or she found on the floor near the copy machine, what would you do? What would you do if you found the copy of the test yourself?

How did Kurt's story make you feel about him? Do you think any more or less of him because of the situation?

Chapter 6

"What saves a man is to take a step.
Then another step."

– *Antoine de Saint-Exupéry*

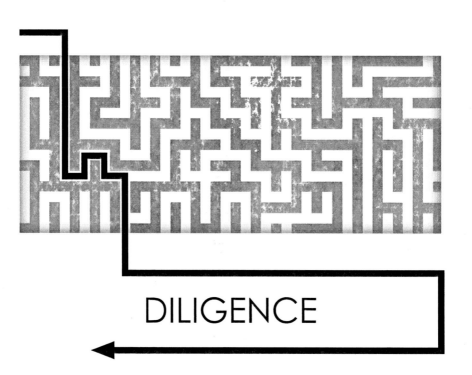

DILIGENCE

Baby Steps

Most of us can't remember the first obstacles we had to overcome in life or how we did it. I can't remember learning to walk or talk or even read. With the help of teachers or parents, we tackled each task and moved onto the next step in life or the next milestone. But in researching the word diligence for this book, I began to think differently about how hard some people have to work to master what many of us consider simple achievements. People like Nina.

Nina has dyslexia, a condition in which people have difficulty recognizing and understanding written words. Her parents call it a learning difference or learning difficulty. She's smart but her brain works differently. While some kids can quickly understand the sound and order of letters in a word, Nina mixes that up. For example, she'll mix up the 'b' and 'd' because they look the same to her.

When Nina was in first grade, her parents didn't realize that Nina couldn't read, because she acted like she could. Her mom said, "Nina would come home with her book. She would read the entire story to me. Only she wasn't really reading it. When her teacher had read the book aloud in class, Nina had memorized it. So at home, she would turn the pages and tell the story…but she wasn't reading the words; she just remembered the story. And I think she thought that was reading. She was only six years old; she didn't know any better…and I was fooled at first. She was just faking us all out."

But in second grade, Nina's problem with reading started causing problems in other areas of her life. Kids would make fun of her and call her stupid. She often came home crying and didn't want to go back to school. At night, she would struggle with her homework, but at the end of a difficult day, she always wanted her parents to read to her. They didn't realize that she wanted to listen to someone who could untangle the words so they made sense.

At first, her parents couldn't figure out what was wrong. They didn't know why she was so tired and was having so much trouble at school. As her mom said, "There is no blood test for a learning disability."

Finally, after seeing a lot of specialists and taking a lot of tests, they figured it out. And that was just the beginning. There is no pill for dyslexia – no quick fix that will make it easier. So Nina's struggle continued, one word at a time, one hour at a time, one day at a time.

She has been struggling with words since the first grade, but now, in high school, she is doing much better. Still, reading is tough. She has to work harder than other kids to learn any subject that requires a lot of reading. She gets extra time to take her tests and some other accommodations at school to help her with her learning difference, but what comes so easily to some of us is still a very difficult task for Nina. "I'm not like some of the other kids. They can pass their tests by studying for a couple of hours, but I have to study all night." She pauses and then says, "It will definitely take me longer to get to my goals, but I just have to remind myself to work hard. I can't be lazy. I have to constantly remind myself to do the work." The key, she says, is concentrating, going slowly, and understanding each word and sentence before she moves on to the next.

Sound familiar? It does to me. I read pretty well, but I can't tell you how many times I've rushed through an exam, reading too fast to really understand the question. And when I go fast, I make stupid mistakes. Like in math. I'll understand the problem and know how to solve it (sometimes), but I will add up 16 and 7 and get 24. That little error makes my whole answer wrong. The difference between Nina and me is that sometimes I am lazy. Because I never had to struggle when I was little, I'll skip steps and try to take shortcuts rather than patiently work through the details to make sure that I do my absolute best.

But Nina learned in second grade that there are no shortcuts. She had to do the work, and for that reason, she says, "Having dyslexia has been a blessing. It's definitely made me a strong-willed person. I look at challenges now, and if it is something that interests me, then I say to myself, 'Let's do it. Let's go for it.'" She says that when you overcome a problem one step at a time, you feel like you can pretty much take on anything. "I totally feel lucky having a learning issue. Do I wish some days that I didn't? Definitely, but if I had to do it over again, I'd probably still pick it. My dyslexia makes me realize that I shouldn't take anything for granted, including my education, and I feel bad for people who walk through life having no idea how lucky they are."

I read somewhere that language, our ability to create it, read it, and write it, may be one of the main characteristics that separates us from other animals. But there are many other traits too. One of those is the internal drive to overcome our difficulties in understanding something; humans have the patience, persistence, and diligence it takes to conquer a challenge.

"People who face adversity early in their lives often learn a skill that will help them achieve lifelong success."

People who face adversity early in their lives often learn a skill that will help them achieve lifelong success. Woodrow Wilson, Albert Einstein, Winston Churchill, and Thomas Edison all struggled with a learning difference and had the advantage of discovering early that there are no shortcuts when it comes to developing greatness.

Discussion/Self-Reflection Questions

1. What is diligence? How do you define it?

2. In the story, Chandler talks about a girl named Nina. How did Nina show diligence?

3. Why do you think Nina didn't give up? What's the reward for being diligent?

4. On a scale of one to ten (ten being the most important and one being least important), how important do you think diligence is as a character trait? Why?

5. Has there been a situation in your own life where you showed diligence in order to overcome something difficult? Explain. How did that feel?

6. Has there been a time when you didn't show as much diligence as you could have? What happened? Is there something you wish you would have done differently?

7. Are there activities that you are involved in now (e.g. sports, math, etc.) where you are being diligent? What helps you stay focused and diligent?

8. What are some things that can get in the way of being diligent?

9. Is diligence learned or are some people just born that way? What are some ways that we can learn to be more diligent?

Journaling Activity

In the childhood book The Little Engine that Could, "I think I can, I think I can," was a common refrain. How can your expectations for yourself impact diligence...and ultimately your accomplishments? What does attitude have to do with diligence?

Sometimes we learn as much from failure as from success. Describe a situation in which you learned from failure – and how diligence played a role (or didn't) in helping you rebound and face the next challenge.

We often hear about the effects of peer pressure, both positive and negative. Can you describe a scenario (real or fictional) in which peer pressure relates to diligence? What was the outcome?

Chapter 7

"Most powerful is he who has
himself in his own power."

– *Seneca*

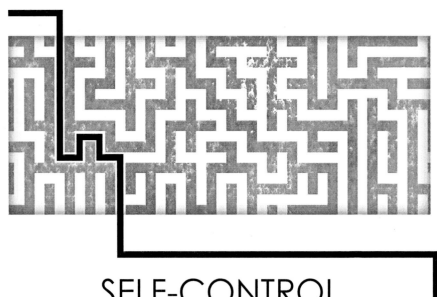

SELF-CONTROL

The Core Four

It was the summer after my senior year of high school. I had made it through!

My parents had always insisted that I not drink while I was in high school. It's not as if they had asked me to never take a sip of alcohol in my life—they enjoyed an occasional beer or glass of wine—but the big message at our house was: delay. Stay away from alcohol in high school.

I had grown up on a steady diet of talks about what I like to call the core four. While some kids and their parents discussed current events at the dinner table, my family's meal conversation often involved the latest story about some kid who had ruined his or her life through sex, drugs, alcohol, or technology. Since my parents produced documentaries on these issues, my brother and I were over-informed on the problems associated with drinking, drugging, having sex, and blasting your business all over Facebook. And I had done what they had asked. I had followed their rules and advice when it came to these issues...that is, until the summer after my senior year.

Among the core four, alcohol was the most tempting. A lot of people I knew started drinking by the time they were sophomores, and most were making good grades and doing just fine. It was hard not to drink – to be one of the few sober kids at a party or concert or not to go at all. I think my parents knew alcohol was going to be the biggest issue for me, so they talked about it almost constantly. And some of what they said actually stuck and had an impact.

I understood that underage drinking was illegal and you could get in serious trouble – arrested, suspended from school, etc. But there was something else that made even more of an impression on me. Both my parents explained that they had had high school friends who drank heavily. Their friends' behavior didn't seem so bad during high school, but many of them became functioning alcoholics; as adults, they still needed a drink to get through any mildly difficult situation. They didn't just drink socially; they drank because they still felt a need to. They drank because they had learned as teenagers that alcohol helped them get over feeling socially awkward or lonely or out of place. So now, as adults, when they felt bad, they drank to feel better. They didn't know any other way. They were dependent on alcohol, possibly forever. Of course, no one had predicted that when they had been kids. My parents didn't want that to happen to me, they said.

That made sense to me and was probably the biggest reason I didn't want to drink in high school. To be honest, I was shy when I was younger, especially in a big group of people. Alcohol could have been an easy way for me to dull that feeling, but I worried, like my parents warned, that if I got in the habit of using alcohol to feel comfortable around people, in the end my shyness would only become worse.

Everybody feels awkward the first time they go to a party or go on a date or meet new people. If you use alcohol to ease the nervousness in those situations, it's a crutch you may start to depend on the rest of your life. I knew I needed to get over being shy, without the use of a substance. So, until the end of my senior year, I had followed my parents' advice.

But now I had graduated, it was the middle of the summer, and some very good friends of mine were having a small party. I knew people were sneaking vodka out of their houses and there would be some drinking – but not in excess. This was a crowd that kept things under control. I planned to spend the night because the party was pretty far away from my house. I was going to ride down to the party with one friend, Sarah, and get a ride back to work the next morning with another girl who was spending the night too. And – oh yeah – I was working for my parents. In fact, I was right in the middle of working on this book. I was feeling pretty independent – out of high school – on my way to college.

My mom was working late, so I didn't see her before Sarah picked me up. I texted her that I planned to spend the night out and would see both my parents at work in the morning. And then I got a phone call… from my dad. He said, "You can't spend the night out tonight because you have to be at work at eight o'clock in the morning. You need to come home."

Excuse me, I thought. Did I just hear him right? He was telling me no! I was 18 years old. I was furious, more ticked off than I had ever been at my parents. I couldn't believe they were pulling this power play, but, I knew better than to challenge my dad, so I said, "Okay," hung up the phone, and called my mom. Surely, she would help me manage around him on this one.

"Mom, what's going on?" I asked. "Dad is saying I can't sleepover at Courtney's. Katherine is going to bring me home in the morning, so I will be at work on time."

I expected her to be sympathetic, but instead she said, "Sorry, Dad's right. You're not staying at someone else's house and staying up until two or three in the morning when you have to work tomorrow. By the way, who is home at Courtney's house – are her parents there?"

Okay – now this was over the top. *Who is home at Courtney's house? Was she kidding me? They were still checking up on me and asking stuff like that, and I had graduated,* I thought. I was annoyed beyond belief. "Mom, come on!" I said. "Courtney's sister is there. I don't know where her parents are, but that shouldn't be any big deal. I've never gotten in any trouble. You can trust me. You know I am responsible."

"Well," she said, "it's true that you've been pretty responsible, but you're still coming home. You need to be here by midnight."

Then I started yelling, "But I am 18! My curfew is 1:00 a.m.! I don't have to be in at midnight anymore."

"Not tonight," she said. "You're working tomorrow, and if you push me, you'll be home by ten, even if I have to come down there and pick you up myself."

I slammed down the phone. This was the thanks I got for following the rules, for being a good kid all through high school and doing what they asked. Well, I was done. It was a new game now.

I told Sarah what had happened and that she was going to have to drive me home from the party, which created another problem because Sarah would have to drive out of her way to take me home, and she had a curfew too. So we were going to have to leave Courtney's house early, which would give us very little time at the party. Sarah was mad. I was mad. And since I wasn't driving, I decided to get even. I would show my parents just what they were dealing with now and that they couldn't control me anymore. It was time to have a drink. They were worried about me being tired at work tomorrow? Well, how about hung over? Let's see if that would be any better. What was the worst they could do?

At the party, I grabbed some vodka and mixer and started to pour. I let go of all my inhibitions, and in one hour, I partied like I never had before. Fortunately, Sarah was smarter than I was, and she wasn't drinking. At the end of the hour, she guided me to the car, shoved me in the passenger seat, and hauled me home. Mom was waiting.

I walked slowly in the house, glassy-eyed, I'm sure, but managed not to stumble. Mom looked at me with a critical eye, gave me a hug, and told me to go to bed.

The next morning, she didn't let the alarm clock wake me up. Instead, she gently nudged me, and when I opened my eyes, she was standing over me holding two ibuprofens and a cup of coffee. "Hung over?" she asked. I rolled my eyes. "You need to get up," she said. "I've taken the morning off work, so you and I can spend a little time together. You can go in late as well."

Oh, no, I thought, *a fate almost worse than death was coming.* I felt like crap, had cottonmouth and a banging headache, and now I had to sit through the third-degree talk with my mom. I was certain it was going to be a long, deep conversation about my actions and choices and how much they would impact the rest of my life. And it was probably going to last hours.

Off we went to breakfast – my head still pounding. The ibuprofen didn't seem to be working. Mom talked and I listened. Some things she said made sense, and this was probably the most important: "Chandler, it's not about the substance, the alcohol. It's about why you drink, the choices you make, and how you handle and manage your moods, emotions, and yourself in difficult situations. And the bottom line is that you didn't have much self-control last night."

> "Did I need to hear again that the real test of who you are doesn't come when you get what you want but how you act when you don't get what you want?"

That part was true. Did I need to hear again that the real test of who you are doesn't come when you get what you want but how you act when you don't get what you want? Did I need to hear that that's when you find out how strong, mature, and solid you are? Maybe so.

I still thought my parents had been heavy-handed and that they were too controlling, particularly given my age and past history of responsible behavior. And reflecting back on even some of the stories in this book, my choices and their consequences could have been a lot worse.

But, I had acted like a spoiled child and had thrown my own little tantrum of sorts. I had let my anger control me and had shown no self-control and not much respect for my parents or for Sarah, who had to drive me home. I had made a stupid choice in order to make a point with my parents. Most high-functioning adults try their best not to do that. I was 18 with one foot out the door, but I still had a lot to learn.

Discussion/Self-Reflection Questions

1. What does it mean to have self-control? How do you define it? Why is self-control important?

2. Chandler writes, "I knew I needed to get over being shy on my own, without the use of a substance." Do you agree with this statement? Why/Why not?

3. Chandler talks about her anger getting the best of her and losing self-control. In what situations do you find it most difficult to show self-control? Explain.

4. Have there been times in your life when you didn't show self-control? What happened? Is there something you wish you would have done differently?

5. Is self-control something you're born with or do you learn it? Explain.

6. What are some ways that someone can improve his or her self-control?

7. Has there been a time in your life when you did show self-control in a difficult situation? How did you do it? What did you learn about yourself? How did it make you feel?

8. Are there times when you can show too much self-control? What does that look like? What might be the down side?

9. Can you think of someone in your life who shows a good balance of self-control and spontaneity? Explain why you think he or she is a good example.

Journaling Activity

Instant messaging. Instant coffee. Instant replay. Our society is one of instant gratification. How does this impact the character trait of self-control? Are our challenges greater today than in the past?

It has been said that everything we need to know we learned in kindergarten. Create a list of ten tips from kindergarten that can help people of any age develop self-control.

Young children are often placed in time-out to help them think about and gain control of their behavior. Create, name, and write about a teen version of time-out. Where would you go? What would you do?

Seneca, a first-century Roman philosopher, wrote, "Most powerful is he who has himself in his own power." Who and/or what influences the power you have in your life? How does that make you feel?

Dale Wimbrow's poem "Guy in the Glass," begins this section of the book. How does this poem relate to self-control? Do you see a person with self-control when you look in the mirror? Explain.

II

Inside Your Community

Desiderata

Go placidly amid the noise and the haste,
and remember what peace there may be in silence.
As far as possible, without surrender,
be on good terms with all persons.
Speak your truth quietly and clearly;
and listen to others,
even to the dull and the ignorant;
they too have their story.
Avoid loud and aggressive persons;
they are vexatious to the spirit.
If you compare yourself with others,
you may become vain or bitter,
for always there will be greater and lesser persons than yourself.
Enjoy your achievements as well as your plans.
Keep interested in your own career, however humble;
it is a real possession in the changing fortunes of time.
Exercise caution in your business affairs,
for the world is full of trickery.
But let this not blind you to what virtue there is;
many persons strive for high ideals,
and everywhere life is full of heroism.
Be yourself. Especially do not feign affection.
Neither be cynical about love,
for in the face of all aridity and disenchantment,
it is as perennial as the grass.
Take kindly the counsel of the years,
gracefully surrendering the things of youth.
Nurture strength of spirit to shield you in sudden misfortune.
But do not distress yourself with dark imaginings.
Many fears are born of fatigue and loneliness.
Beyond a wholesome discipline,
be gentle with yourself.

You are a child of the universe
no less than the trees and the stars;
you have a right to be here.
And whether or not it is clear to you,
no doubt the universe is unfolding as it should.
Therefore be at peace with God,
whatever you conceive Him to be.
And whatever your labors and aspirations,
in the noisy confusion of life,
keep peace in your soul.
With all its sham, drudgery, and broken dreams,
it is still a beautiful world.
Be cheerful. Strive to be happy.

– *Max Ehrmann*

Chapter 8

"The true meaning of life is to plant trees, under whose shade you do not expect to sit."

– Nelson Henderson

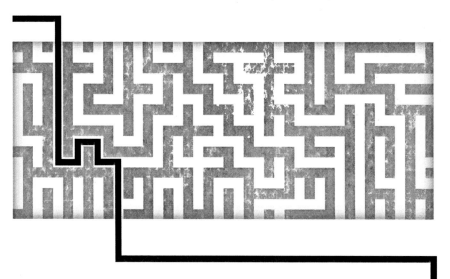

CARING/COMPASSION

One Last Gift

I sometimes question whether there is fairness in the world. If there is, it may be too complicated a mystery for me to understand. If things were fair and just, then why would bad things happen to good people, sometimes to very good people? In one instance, the bad thing was very bad and the good person was a friend of mine. She helped me remember something that I too often forget: what's important and what isn't. And how good can come out of horrible tragedy if we only look inside ourselves and those around us.

It was the beginning of summer after my junior year. School had just let out and my friends and I were enjoying that rush of freedom you feel when you first get out for summer vacation. You know what I mean. It's part illusion (I mean you still have to do things at home, and worry about a summer job, the summer reading list, a curfew, and lots of questions from your parents). But for a few hours, it's great!

On this morning, we were all texting – making plans about what time to meet that night, where and when we were shopping over the weekend, and which day to spend at the pool. But then, in the middle of my last text, the phone rang and I got the news. Alex, a girl in my class, had died. Plans were being made for her memorial service. Could I come? Would I spread the word? What happened? Who knew? All these questions were flying back and forth.

Word was spreading fast. I walked to my computer and logged onto Facebook as I listened to my friend's rapid recall of what she had been told about Alex's death. My Facebook page was already inundated with messages. Almost the entire class had signed on and sent messages grieving the loss or comforting her family.

Alex was a friend of mine, a girl I had known throughout high school. She was seventeen years old, a junior like me; thin, pale, and pretty with blonde hair and a bright smile. She had been living with a rare, incurable illness since the day she was born. She told me about the disease one time. It was genetic. She inherited it. She said the disease caused a lot of pain, congestion in her lungs, and trouble breathing. She had lots of infections and was in and out of hospitals for most of her life. Still, she went to school every day and made friends, studied, and tried to live as normal a life as possible even though she and her family knew that her life would most likely be shorter than that of most kids her age.

I got to know Alex through one of the programs at my school. It was a discussion group where you'd meet kids and talk about the deeper meaning of life. Each meeting had a theme – like about being honest, about the "masks" we wear to hide our feelings and fears from others, and about how tough or competitive or challenging it is to be a teenager (and sometimes how great it is, too). Part of the time we had long conversations, and part of the time kept open to reflect, to think quietly about what we heard in each discussion. And in each meeting, we were reminded by the group leaders that we all had to support each other.

Alex made a huge effort to come to these meetings. She missed a lot of school because of her sickness. There were times when she could barely walk because breathing was so difficult, but she tried as hard as she could not to miss our sessions. If I didn't feel like going because I was tired and just wanted to chill, I thought of her. She said the program gave her strength to hang in there against such a debilitating disease.

I remember that during these meetings, Alex would say she thought there must be a plan for all of us. Even though it was hard for her to understand why she was sick and why she had to endure this suffering, Alex always trusted that there was some purpose, some reason for her illness and that it would be apparent one day. She was amazing! She suffered almost daily, but wasn't bitter about her disease. The way she handled herself through the tough times made her an inspiration to all of us. She was quiet, mostly, but positive, energetic, and pretty smart. But, that is not why people stopped and listened when she said something. We stopped talking and turned toward Alex when she spoke because she knew something the rest of us didn't. When she talked about life, about the meaning of why we were here and what we were supposed to do during our lives to help others, her perspective was different from ours. Alex knew she would probably die young. She seemed more thoughtful and serious than most our age. And, I got the impression that she never lied. She didn't exaggerate and never made up stuff. That's one of the reasons I liked her. No games. No drama.

Still, even though Alex knew and we knew that she might live a shorter life than the rest of us, her death came as a surprise. It happened suddenly, in a moment, without warning. Her family was with her. She had told them she wasn't feeling well, and she thought she needed to get to a hospital. Alex was really tuned into how she felt physically each day, so she could usually tell when something inside of her wasn't right. Her family called an ambulance and rushed her to a nearby hospital, but not in time.

It was difficult for those of us who knew her because we never got a chance to say goodbye. Some people call it closure. The idea is that people need an ending. If something bad happens, like the death of somebody you love, you can't just have them with you one day and then have somebody call you the next day and say they're gone. You need to say goodbye.

At the funeral, when her parents gave the eulogy, Alex's mom told everyone that she asked Alex what made her happy. Her answer was our monthly meetings, when we talked about life. When I heard that, my friend Lindsey grabbed my hand and we both lost it. The program was very special to us, and to hear how Alex had felt about it was overwhelming.

During the funeral, I let my mind wander, remembering who Alex had been and what she had been like. She always spoke her mind—carefully—and she always looked around the room as she talked to see if the looks on our faces showed that we understood what she had been trying to say. Alex was an original. I realized her strength had influenced me. I sat there, half listening, looking at the flowers, with tears in my eyes thinking how much I would miss her.

We were all devastated by the news, but instead of grieving alone, we formed a kind of community and decided to do something for Alex, her family, and each other. When you feel that much sadness, you need to do something with it. You can't ignore it or just let it sit there inside of you. My friend Elizabeth took it upon herself to organize a candlelight memorial for Alex on our school campus. One evening, with the lights kept low, with our faces lit by a shining candle that each of us held in our hands, almost every student in the school gathered to hold a prayer service for Alex. And each of us wore a green ribbon, because that was her favorite color.

Later that week, we made posters with pictures and stories and a few words about how we felt about Alex. We all signed the boards and gave them to her parents. We wanted them to know how much we cared and that we felt their sadness and their pain. I think maybe, when you care for someone who is sick, and they're sick for years and years, and in their struggle you see how brave they are, you get really close to them. And it hurts more than anything when they're gone.

Before the funeral and for a while afterwards, people banded together to help Alex's family. Families mowed the lawn and raked leaves and ran errands for them. People made dozens of meals and delivered them to the house so they didn't have to worry about grocery shopping or cooking or cleaning up the dishes when they were so filled with grief. On their front porch, people left bouquets, baskets filled with fruit and candy, and all kinds of food, cards, and letters. And I had a chance to see what happens when small acts of kindness are multiplied by dozens of people. It's contagious. And all of it was a kind of code. A simple, silent message from all of us that we missed Alex, and we loved her, and somehow we hoped that comforted her family.

All this for a girl who in some ways appeared to be ordinary, but who had an extraordinary impact on an entire community. She loved going to school, loved long talks with her friends, really enjoyed those monthly meetings, and liked making new friends. She liked to yell at football and basketball games and yet, every day, she was in pain fighting a cruel and fatal disease.

"We were one community bonded by something much bigger than ourselves." All the kids in my school were never more together than we were when we united for Alex. No disagreements, no sarcasm or jokes or quick one-liners making fun of someone. No competition or fighting over some guy or girl. No jealousy or meanness. Not then. All of that seemed really stupid, out of place, and unimportant. In that moment of hearing the news of her death and the days that followed, we started to reveal the best parts of our selves. We were one community bonded by something much bigger than ourselves. Thanks to Alex. It was her last gift to us.

Discussion/Self-Reflection Questions

1. In the chapter, Chandler says, "I had the chance to see what happens when small acts of caring are multiplied by dozens of people." Can you think of a small act of caring that someone has shown for you? What did it mean to you?

2. Can you think of a time when you showed an act of caring for someone else? Explain. How did it also benefit you?

3. Do you think caring and compassion are common or rare behaviors in our society? Explain.

4. Chandler and her friends honored Alex by wearing green, which was her favorite color. What does it mean to honor someone? Why is it important?

5. Do you think the caring and compassion shown by Alex's friends made a difference to her family? Why/Why not?

6. Chandler describes Alex as a girl, who in many ways was ordinary, but inspired a whole community to come together. What do you think led to this outpouring of caring and compassion?

7. It seems, from this story, that caring and compassion can be contagious. Do you think that's true? What does that say about our actions in society? Explain.

8. What did Chandler say about what made Alex different from other people? Do you think those are rare qualities in a person? Explain.

9. Chandler talks about the togetherness she felt with her friends at the funeral. Who do you reach out to for caring and support when you're going through a tough time? How does it make a difference?

10. The chapter begins with the Nelson Henderson quote, "The true meaning of life is to plant trees, under whose shade you do not expect to sit." How do you think this quote relates to Chandler's story of care and compassion?

Journaling Activity

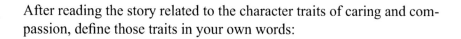

After reading the story related to the character traits of caring and compassion, define those traits in your own words:

The chapter begins with the quote: "The true meaning of life is to plant trees, under whose shade you do not expect to sit." Let's say you were provided $100,000 to show caring or compassion for anyone or anything, anywhere in the world. Describe below what you would do. What could you do that would involve no money at all?

At Alex's memorial service, her mom said that the monthly meetings with her friends made Alex happy. In the space below, write about what makes you happy. Do you think others know this about you?

Chandler states that the littlest act of caring can make a difference. Describe specific ways that you can show more caring and compassion in your own life as it relates to your school, friends, family, community, etc.

Chapter 9

"I'll take fifty percent efficiency to get one hundred percent loyalty."

– Samuel Goldwyn

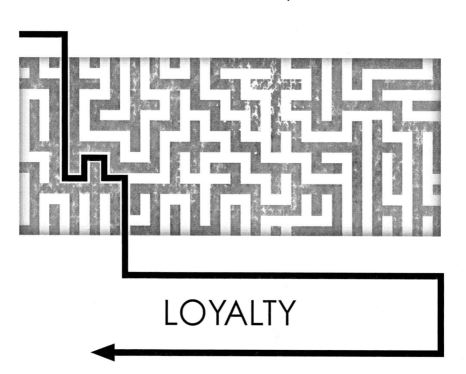

LOYALTY

Being in the Room with It

Some musicians call it "being in the room with it." It's a slang phrase for the energy or mood that is created when musicians and their audiences connect and the music takes on a life of its own. At that point, it is no longer about who is onstage or the performance or applause – the music just takes over. At least, that's how a family friend, a drummer who has been into music his whole life, described it to me. And, it is definitely a feeling I can relate to.

I love music, but I have no special talent for it. I play the guitar and sing a little, but I am just an average singer: decent voice, limited range, no great ability. If you want a lot of voices to add volume and fill up a room, that's where I can help. So, in my junior year of high school, I joined the chorus.

At my school, you could take three trimesters of chorus each year, but most kids took it for only one or two. It was a fun class but not something you would generally stay with unless you were really into singing or performing and were pretty good at it. Since I was neither, most people, including my chorus teacher and me, expected me to fall into the one-trimester crowd. I stood on the back row, sang alto, and occasionally missed high notes, low notes, and some in between. At the end of my first trimester, I tried out for the advanced chorus and didn't make it. My voice wasn't strong enough. All of my friends who were staying in the class did make the advanced chorus or the trios, quartets, and other elite singing groups. That meant that if I were going to take a second trimester, I would actually be singing with a younger group during a different period.

But I looked forward to the class every day, not because my friends were in it, but because I just really enjoyed being part of a chorus. I didn't care if I was on the back row. I learned to sing and to read music, and that was something I always wanted to do.   It helped me with guitar.

For me, music is unlike anything else in life. It touches a different part of the brain. It has a power that connects people on a different level. Whether it's a century-old hymn or some version of a popular song, the sound that comes from a group of people singing their individual parts or harmonies moves me.

So I decided to sign up for a second trimester and then a third. I eventually ended up taking chorus for six trimesters – my entire junior and senior years – even though it meant I didn't have room in my schedule to take some other electives that I wanted, including creative writing and drawing. I went to chorus class every day, and I went to rehearsals and concerts. I tried not to miss anything. I never advanced to the higher level, and for two years, I stayed on the back row. No awards, no honors. I didn't care; I just liked the class.

Then graduation was approaching. It was the end of my senior year and the night of the spring concert, an event where a lot of the seniors perform individually or in a small group. It's sort of a like a last opportunity for them to showcase their talent. I had always loved watching that part of the show but had no interest in participating, so I was just part of the bigger numbers that involved the whole group.

> "I never advanced to the higher level, and for two years, I stayed on the back row. No awards, no honors. I didn't care; I just liked the class."

As was the tradition, at the end of the concert, our choral director gave out the annual awards to the outstanding junior, outstanding trio singer, outstanding chamber choir member, and many others. The winners walked to the front of the stage as the audience applauded. Then it was time for the outstanding senior award. Our teacher said, "This year, I am giving this award to a person who is steady and consistent. She has been in chorale for six trimesters and stands in the back row. If I'm having a bad day or things seem a little out of sorts, I can walk in and see her smiling face. I look up and know she's there…and I know we're good to go. This year's outstanding senior award goes to…"

And I heard my name. What? My face was on fire. I was in shock. My boyfriend, who was standing nearby, was applauding like crazy and laughing at me. I couldn't believe it. I'm not sure that anyone else could believe it either. Afterwards, my parents, who were in the audience, said they were in shock too. I will never forget that moment.

There were many other seniors who could have received that award – people who never sang off-key, loved performing, and were going to study music in college – but the chorus director said I deserved it because of my dedication and loyalty to the program. And I was loyal, not only to the program, but to the music, to my passion, to the activity I enjoyed. I loved just "being in the room with it."

Discussion/Self-Reflection Questions

1. What does loyalty mean to you? How important is this character trait to you?

2. The chapter begins with the term "being in the room with it." Have you ever experienced that feeling? When? What was it like?

3. Chandler writes about being loyal not only to the program but to her passion for music. Do you have a passion for something? What is it? What does it mean to be loyal to developing discipline around your passion? Is that what Chandler did when she was loyal to the program?

4. Can you describe a situation in which you have demonstrated loyalty? Explain.

5. Can you describe a situation in which someone has been loyal to you? How did that make you feel?

6. Describe a situation in which your loyalty, perhaps to a friend, has gotten you in trouble. Was it worth it?

7. Why do you think schools create award ceremonies to recognize students? Do you believe the recognition accomplishes its goal(s)?

8. How does the quote at the beginning of the chapter, "I'll take fifty percent efficiency to get one hundred percent loyalty," relate to Chandler's story?

Journaling Activity

The phrase "fair-weather fan" refers to someone who disappears at the first sign of trouble. Sports fans can be a loyal or disloyal bunch. Take on the role of a sportswriter and critique the fans at a school or community sporting event. Observe and describe their loyalty.

What to you believe it the most important quality in a friend? Where does loyalty rank?

The men and women of our armed forces demonstrate a special brand of loyalty. Write a letter to someone who has enlisted. Share your feelings about his or her demonstration of loyalty to our country.

Imagine that you have launched a business. Describe the ways you will encourage loyalty among your employees – and why this is important to your success.

This section of the book begins with the Max Ehrmann poem "Desiderata." How do the lines "Enjoy your achievements as well as your plans. Keep interested in your own career, however humble; it is a real possession in the changing fortunes of time," relate to this story and to the word loyalty?

Chapter 10

"Being considerate of others will take your children further in life than any college degree."

– *Marian Wright Edelman*

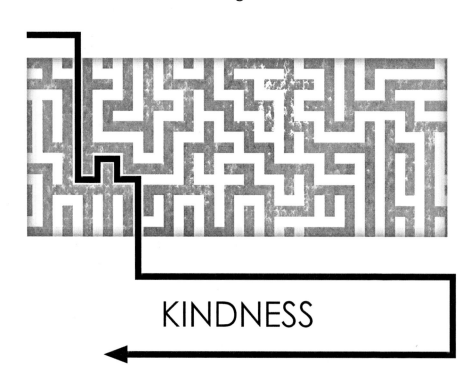

KINDNESS

The Gentle Giant

I have a friend named Carlos. He was a pretty big deal at my high school. He's was one of the stars on our football team and well-known in our city's sports community because our team won at least 90 percent of its games and was ranked number 1 or 2 in the conference every year.

During football season, Carlos and the rest of the starting players were spotlighted in the local newspaper most weekends. Halfway through his freshman year, Carlos became and continued to be the concrete block at the center of our offensive line. You might think somebody like that would be arrogant or stuck up, but not Carlos. He was laidback, funny, and smart. Everybody liked him and said he was like a big teddy bear, giant in size, personality, and heart. He was not afraid to be himself.

But enough about Carlos. There's another kid I want to tell you about. His name was Kobe. He was a foreign exchange student from Africa who came to my school after his mother had died from AIDS and his father had left him. Kobe has experienced more pain and suffering in his first 16 years than most of us will in a lifetime. He had been taking care of his brothers and sisters back in Africa, but when he was given a once-in-a-lifetime chance to finish high school in the United States, his brothers and sisters went to live with cousins, and he came to my school.

It wasn't easy for Kobe. His host family lived pretty far away from school. To get to class every day, Kobe rode his bike to a subway station, took the commuter train (with his bicycle and books on board), and then got off the train and biked the rest of the way to school. It took him over 90 minutes each way, but he didn't complain. He said he was just grateful for the opportunity to be here, learn English, and study in an American school. A lot of kids back in his home village would have done almost anything to have gotten an education, but they had very little money and not many books, teachers, or schools. Who Kobe was and what he did each day amazed me, and sometimes I felt bad about all that I had and all that he didn't.

But I later came to realize that Kobe had a lot, not necessarily in material things, but in his spirit; in his ability to handle situations with grace, courage, and calmness; and in his upbeat attitude and willingness to try new things.

When Kobe first came to my school, I often saw him sitting by himself at lunch. No one was really reaching out to be his friend (including me). I'm embarrassed to admit that we were so wrapped up in our own lives, our own friends, and our classes, that we really didn't think about how to include Kobe.

It also took a lot of effort to talk to Kobe. His English was not very good, and he was difficult to understand, but that never stopped him from going to dances and football games. And wherever he went, he was smiling. And little by little, his English improved.

Many weeks later, when the students and teachers went on a weekend retreat, which was a great opportunity to leave our worries at home, I noticed that Kobe and Carlos had found each other, and they made quite a contrasting pair. Kobe was so short and skinny that you would have thought Carlos would have knocked him down if he had thrown Kobe a football.

On the retreat, Carlos took Kobe under his wing, including him in everything he did with his friends and spending a lot of one-on-one time with him too. They went for runs together during free time and ate breakfast, lunch, and dinner together. Carlos also encouraged his friends to get to know Kobe better. I know Kobe appreciated the kindness. It was the first time he really felt included.

> "By watching Carlos, I learned that reaching out to someone, even if that person is way out of your comfort zone, can be very rewarding."

As people witnessed what Carlos was doing, they also started to connect with Kobe. By the end of the weekend, just about everyone, including me, looked upon Kobe as a friend.

By watching Carlos, I learned that reaching out to someone, even if that person is way out of your comfort zone, can be very rewarding. I discovered that even though Kobe and I were very different in language, personality, culture, and religion, we also shared similarities. We both had a desire to be accepted by the people around us.

At the end of the retreat, Kobe gave each of us a personal letter thanking us for our friendship. Reading his words, we had tears in our eyes because we were so touched by what Kobe said; he had found something of value in each one of us. And everyone knew that we had Carlos to thank for the way we felt that weekend.

When we got back to school, Carlos continued his friendship with Kobe and so did most of us. And, Kobe's life started to change. He met a lot of new people and became much more accepted by everyone all because one person took the lead. One person reached out to a kid. A stranger who was struggling a little bit ended up making a friend. And like other acts of kindness, it grew and spread. Soon it touched others, and more people noticed. In the end, the whole school was better…kinder…than it was before.

Discussion/Self-Reflection Questions

1. What is kindness? How do you define it? How important do you believe kindness is as a character trait?

2. What are little acts of kindness? Why are they important? Can you think of a small act of kindness that someone did for you? What did it mean?

3. The chapter describes the environment at the retreat as one where the students left all their worries at home. Can you think of an environment that makes you feel that way? How and why might that have a positive impact on kindness?

4. What do you think motivated Carlos to reach out to Kobe when it would have been easier not to? What did he gain from his kind actions?

5. Have you ever reached out to someone like Kobe the way that Carlos did? If so, what made you do it? Was it difficult? What did you gain from the experience? Explain.

6. Do you see yourself as a leader, like Carlos, in taking the first steps towards reaching out to others and being kind, or are you more likely to follow someone else's actions? Explain.

7. Kobe gave each one of the kids on the retreat a personal letter thanking them for their friendship. Do you think it matters whether or not kindness is recognized?

8. At the end of the chapter, Chandler writes that Carlos was given the right name. What do you think she means by that?

9. The chapter begins with this quote from Marian Wright Edelman: Being considerate of others will take your children further in life than any college degree. Who is Marian Wright Edelman? Does it surprise you that she feels this way? Do you agree?

Journaling Activity

Surely you've heard the phrase: The way to a person's heart is through his or her stomach! Let's take that literally. Create a recipe for kindness.

Take this kindness challenge. Do one act of kindness every day for a week. Write down the reactions of others…and how they made you feel.

John F. Kennedy wrote, "I am certain that after the dust of centuries has passed over our cities, we, too, will be remembered not for victories or defeats in battle or in politics, but for our contributions to the human spirit." What would you like written about your contributions to the human spirit?

Write about a time you experienced the kindness – or a lack thereof – of others. Did that experience change you in any way? Explain.

The beginning of this book begins with the poem "The Road Not Taken" by Robert Frost. How do you believe this poem relates to the character trait of kindness?

Chapter 11

"If you can't feed a hundred people,
then just feed one."

– *Mother Teresa*

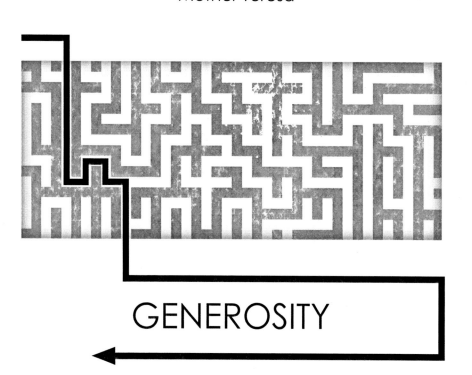

GENEROSITY

Time for Tina

Sometimes school is boring. There's no sense pretending otherwise. When that one teacher goes on and on without a pause or a question or a break, it can be tough-to-keep-your-eyes-open long and dull. It happens. Not with most teachers or most classes but sometimes. (Of course, occasionally it's my fault for staying up way too late and then going to school the next morning with my eyes half open and my brain half asleep.)

Often though, the problem isn't an unexciting class or teacher, or a tired kid. Some kids are bored with and hate school for an entirely different reason. It has nothing to do with intelligence or abilities. It's something else, something that can best be explained by the story of a kid I knew named Tina.

"It started in seventh grade." Tina said. "I was just going through adolescence, and I was lost. I was confused. I didn't know what I wanted to do. I just started acting out in class, hanging out with the wrong crowd. Up until that point, I was a really good student. I always liked language arts and science. Yeah, I was a good kid up until about middle school."

Tina had shiny black hair and big brown eyes, although for a while she wore a lot of dark make-up on those eyes. She was a very unhappy kid.

"I was skipping class a lot," she said. "I hardly ever went to school, and when I did, I think I spent more time in the principal's office than I actually did in class. I was disrespectful to the teachers. I would address them however I wanted to address them, and I was disruptive in class. I would talk to my friends, never pay attention, and cuss out the teachers on a whim, anytime I felt like it."

She ditched school for 30 days during her freshman year in high school, got suspended a bunch of times, and spent so many hours in the waiting room outside the principal's office that they should have reserved a chair for her there with her name painted on it. It had to end, and finally, it did. The principal told her that she had missed too many days to continue, and she would have to go to an alternative high school for kids who were in trouble.

"I felt like nobody was ever going to understand me, that I was going to make nothing of my life, that I was always going to have a dead-end job, and there was no hope. I was never going to get any better," she said. Then she stopped for a second. I could tell it was hard for her to talk about all of this. These were pretty hard years for her. Her eyes started to tear up...she was trying hard not to cry. "I guess I just didn't have any faith in myself," she continued. But she wasn't lost yet. Not quite.

In alternative school, Tina started to turn her life around. Part of that was the result of realizing what could happen if she didn't finish school, but there was something else. She found another reason to stay in school. Or I should say it found her. It was Ms. Sanchez, a part-time language arts teacher and full-time counselor who believed in Tina.

Ms. Sanchez helped lots of kids, not just Tina. Ms. Sanchez explained, "I like to connect with the kids right away. Even just asking, 'How are you? How are you feeling, you look a little sad, what's going on?' As opposed to 'Your teacher told me you're not doing your homework...what's going on?' Just giving them that space, they realize they do count."

I don't know how many students Ms. Sanchez had assigned to her as a counselor, but she gave Tina her time right from the start. Ms. Sanchez said, "I think Tina felt that there was somebody listening to her, that no matter what it was, what problem or crisis, I would be there...listening, still willing to help...and not criticizing or complaining, or making her feel like everything was all her fault and everything she did was wrong."

Tina started handing in her homework. Her grades got better. She stopped missing school. She stopped coming to school tired and angry and gloomy.

"Ms. Sanchez always listened to me," Tina said. "I always felt that of everyone in my life, she understood me the best, and she never gave up on me, even when I tested her to see how she would react. The test was: If I skip school, will you still like me? If I forget to do my home-

91

work or fail a test or come to school late or talk too loud in class, will you still like me, still believe in me? Will you? WILL YOU? And the answer was always yes. There were consequences, detentions, some extra homework, some make-up tests, a few more trips to the principal's office, but the answer was always yes. She was relentless," Tina continued, describing Ms. Sanchez. "I believed that I was a good kid no matter how bad I was acting…because she always tried to tell me that. She would always tell me that I was special, that I had potential, that I was smart, and that I could accomplish things if I just put my mind to it and if I really tried."

You know how this story ends. Or you can guess. Tina graduated. She received a high school diploma. She is now in college, studying to become a social worker. Somebody gave Tina time; now Tina wants to do the same for someone else.

Discussion/Self-Reflection Questions

1. What is generosity? How do you define it?

2. How important is generosity as a character trait? What other character traits might influence or have an impact on generosity?

3. Why did Tina act the way that she did? Explain. Do you know students like Tina? Was there someone there whose generosity helped them through the situation?

4. How did Ms. Sanchez show generosity toward Tina? How did that make a difference in Tina's life?

5. Do you know kids who feel that they don't have a connection or support? How is that affecting their decisions...and their lives? Explain.

6. Have you ever reached out to someone like Tina? Why/Why not? How might school be different if we all did?

7. Is there someone who believes in you and is generous in some way – via his or her time, support, etc.? How does that person's generosity make a difference to you?

8. Besides showing generosity by being there for someone, what are some other ways we can show generosity?

9. The chapter begins with this quote from Mother Teresa: If you can't feed a hundred people, then just feed one. What does this quote mean to you? How does it apply to generosity?

Journaling Activity

Write a generosity manual in which you outline the basic steps for the "Care and Feeding of Your Generosity."

Complete this sentence: To me, generosity looks like…

You have been selected to nominate recipients of a generosity award in your school and your community. Who would you nominate for this award and why?

Unfortunately, too many people are not recognized for their generosity until their death. Read through your local obituaries. What information did you learn about the generosity of people in your community?

Write a letter to thank someone for his or her generosity.

This book begins with Robert Frost's poem "The Road Not Taken." How does this poem relate to generosity?

Chapter 12

"Patience is also a form of action."

– Auguste Rodin

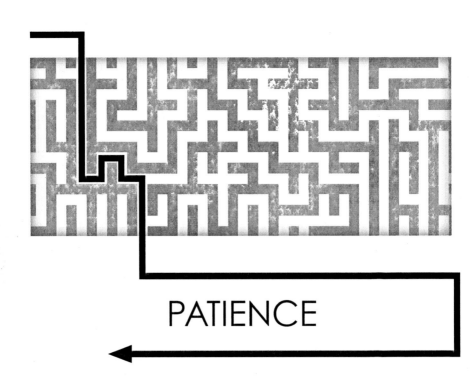

PATIENCE

Seeing the Rewards

Most summers during high school, I worked for my parents' company doing grunt work – logging tapes, filing, answering the phone. But one summer, they decided I needed a real job with a real boss who wasn't related to me and told me to find something else. I was relieved because it's a little difficult to spend all day working with your parents and then living in the same house with them on nights and weekends. So, the summer after my junior year, I applied for and got a job as a camp counselor. That is when I met Camille.

It was my first week of work, and I was assigned to watch the playground during a free period. I was playing chase with one group of girls and boys when off to my side, I noticed a girl jumping rope.

She was in perfect sync, never missing a beat as the little kids around her sang a rhyme, but she looked kind of weird. She was about 9 or 10 and had stringy reddish-brown hair. She seemed more like a tomboy than a girly girl – no bows or purse anywhere around. And, she seemed to be having much more fun than the other kids, giggling out loud and letting out a kind of wild, goofy, scream of joy throughout her turn. But her head was kind of bobbing back and forth; it seemed unnatural. *Was there something wrong with her?* I thought. I walked closer to check it out. Then, I realized she was blind. Wow! I'd never seen a blind person jump rope before, so I stood there staring, something I had been taught not to do, with my mouth half open as she jumped and jumped until someone had to ask her to stop. I asked a returning counselor about this girl who had me mesmerized. She said the child's name was Camille and that Camille had been blind since birth from a condition that kept her eyes from fully developing.

After the free period ended, it was time for arts and crafts. I asked my boss if I could work with Camille. We sat down at the table, and I introduced myself. She asked if I would hand her the colors, glue, construction paper, and scissors as she asked for them. It would save time, she said, and her parents' gift would be so much prettier! So I sat there and handed her stuff and laughed out loud as she pasted up cardboard and construction paper, relying only on her touch and my help. She was hysterical – happy, totally care-free, and easy-going. I didn't see her get frustrated once – no throwing down the scissors, or crying, or slamming her hands on the table. She just patiently glued and colored and drew circles and squares by using cookie cutter shapes that the staff had provided as extra help for her.

That day, when Camille's mother picked her up from camp, I stopped by to talk to her and told her how impressed I was with her daughter. I told her that I had spent time getting to know Camille during arts and crafts after I saw her jumping rope on the playground. Her mother smiled and said, "You know the jump rope changed Camille's life. There is a funny story behind that." She told me that a couple of years earlier, Camille had asked for a jump rope. Apparently, all the other kids in the neighborhood were playing jump rope, and Camille wanted to try it. "We've always tried to treat her as normal as possible, so reluctantly, we bought one for her," her mom recalled.

Every afternoon, Camille would go out in the driveway and try to jump that rope. She would fall, skin her knee, cry, throw the rope on the ground, and yell, "I can't do this!"

And her dad would pick her up, brush her off, and say, "You can do anything with practice and patience."

And so off she would go to try again. Gradually, she got better and better. Her mom said that in a couple of days, Camille ran in the house and shouted, "Look at me. I can jump five times in a row." Then it was 10, and then it was 20, until she developed the rhythm and balance she needed to succeed.

"Now every time she wants to give up, we remind her about the jump rope. With practice and patience you can do anything."

I was amazed. I wondered: How long would I try, how long would I work hard at learning to jump rope if I were blind? Just as the thought entered my mind, Camille's mother said, "Have you ever tried jumping rope with your eyes closed? Not a lot of fun. Give it a try sometime."

That afternoon when I got home, I went down to our basement and pulled out a jump rope. I knew I was pretty good at it with my eyes open. All those competitive sports I had played as a kid paid off when it came to jumping rope. Skipping a hundred times fast with both feet barely skimming the ground is something I can usually do without breaking a sweat. But then I tried it with my eyes closed and couldn't jump more than five times without falling. After about three minutes, I had had enough and decided to watch a little TV instead. Obviously, I had answered my earlier question. I didn't have the patience to practice.

But Camille did. That summer, I spent time with her at work whenever I could. The more I got to know her, the more I liked her. She laughed a lot and had a pretty good sense of humor, but she was actually kind of quiet – not a chatterbox at all. She may not have always said a lot, but she did more than anybody her age. And she taught me that patience is an active word.

Before I met Camille, patience was not one of my better qualities. When I thought about being patient, I thought about sitting and waiting and enduring something I did not want to do. It never occurred to me that patience was a kind of action, a way to persevere, to try something over and over again until you got it right.

I was 16 and she was 9, but Camille understood what I had not yet figured out. She could do almost anything she tried. Not at first, but with patience and practice, she would conquer it: swimming, running a relay, arts and crafts. She brought her unique personality and way of doing things to every task, but she got the job done. We had to make special accommodations for her sometimes and give her extra time, but she was always willing to sit there and work at it no matter how long it took. She intuitively seemed to understand that things were just going to take her a little longer and that she could outlast the difficulty of the problem. And, that's how she conquered everything, using baby steps, one small success at a time. I honestly have never known anyone with as much patience and perseverance as Camille.

> "She intuitively seemed to understand that things were just going to take her a little longer and that she could outlast the difficulty of the problem."

The more time I spent with her, the more I learned. She wasn't just good at camp activities. Apparently, she was pretty good at school as well. She was an A student, played the piano, knew Braille (reading by feeling tiny bumps on the page), and was learning Spanish and Arabic, which was her father's first language. Her parents had taken her rock climbing, whitewater rafting and horseback riding.

Right before camp ended that summer, Camille's older sister sat down beside me at lunch one day and started talking. She was 12, a sixth-grader, three years older than Camille. She was goofing off and laughing and making fun of Camille who was sitting on the other side of me. But Camille was not fazed. She just laughed along with her sister and started teasing her back, particularly about being a chicken. I started to laugh, and her sister insisted, "No, she's right. I am a chicken, at least more chicken than her. I'm like afraid to go surfing because I hate sharks, or at least I'm scared of them. But Camille will go out. She'll go surfing, she'll go whitewater rafting, she'll go rock climbing, and all that stuff." And then with great pride, she continued, "And not only that, my friends and I used to play the 'blind game' with Camille when we were little. We'd like pretend that we were blind and stuff, and we would put blindfolds on to cover our eyes. We would run into so many things, crash into stuff... and then Camille would come out and walk straight to the kitchen and not run into anything, and we'd be like – 'how do you do that?'"

And Camille would answer, "With practice and patience, you can do anything."

Discussion/Self-Reflection Questions

1. What is patience? How do you define it? How important do you believe patience is as a character trait?

2. On a scale of one to ten (one being not at all, ten being extremely), how patient do you think you are? Who or what might help you to be more patient in your life? How would being more patient help you reach your goals?

3. What can we learn from Camille's story? What are its lessons?

4. What are the ways Camille's family offered her encouragement? How do you think that affected her attitude?

5. Can you think of someone in your own life who wasn't patient and couldn't see beyond the present to something better in the future? What happened? Explain. What can you learn from his or her situation?

6. Auguste Rodin was a French sculptor, often considered the progenitor of modern sculpture. His quote, "Patience is also a form of action," begins this chapter. What does this quote mean to you? How is patience a form of action? Do you think people equate patience with laziness?

7. When have you had be patient with yourself? With others? Do you find one more challenging than the other?

8. Think of a time someone lost patience. How did that make you feel?

9. What was the most challenging situation, no matter how trivial, in which you had to demonstrate patience?

10. This section of the book begins with the poem "Desiderata." How do you think this poem relates to the character trait of patience?

Journaling Activity

Rarely do our leaders have the benefit of hindsight. If you could give one piece of advice on being more patient to any person in history, select a historical figure and provide that advice.

It has been said that no job requires more patience than parenting. In what ways do you think you challenge your parents' patience? What kind of parent do you want to be?

Technology – instant messaging, texting, the Internet – makes our access to communication and information almost immediate. In what ways do you believe technology challenges our patience? Is patience becoming a lost art? Do you believe there are benefits to slowing down the pace? Explain.

Chandler's story describes how Camille overcame any obstacles blindness seemed to place in her path. Imagine a world without one of your senses. Describe what your life would be like and what character traits you might call upon to overcome the challenge.

Chapter 13

"Manners are a sensitive awareness of the feelings of others. If you have that awareness, you have good manners, no matter what fork you use."

– Emily Post

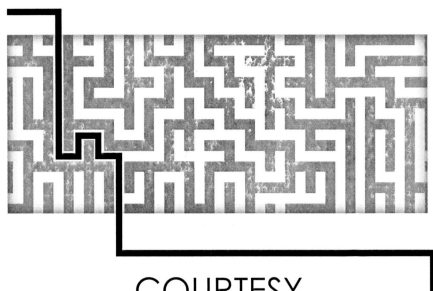

COURTESY

A Grandmother's Wisdom

Throughout high school, when my parents would go out of town, my brother and I would stay with my grandparents. I liked being at their house because they had a tendency to spoil us. My grandmother would buy any food we wanted and let us watch movies all afternoon. I have fond memories of hanging out in my grandfather's workshop and barely being able to peek over the steering wheel when my grandmother let me drive around the church parking lot. They always let us get away with things my parents wouldn't, but just the small things, not the big ones.

One particular weekend during my sophomore year, when I was staying with my grandparents, I was playing around on the computer because my grandmother wanted me to download some of her music to her new iPod. While I was looking for the songs she requested, I noticed that Carrie Underwood, one of my favorite singers, was on the 2006 list of the Ten Best Mannered People, which is published by the National League of Junior Cotillions. *That's pretty cool*, I thought. I didn't even know there was such a list. Something Carrie Underwood said also impressed me. She said, "I want people to think of me as a nice person. I really am so blessed."

Grandmother is always reminding me to be nice and count my blessings. I thought, *Maybe Carrie had a grandmother like mine.* Other things Grandmother says and uses frequently are "Put yourself in their place" or "How would you feel?" There are more, too many to name here, and they all seem to be about compassion, which creates civility, which includes manners, fair play, and how you live your life in general. She calls them Lessons from The Greatest Generation – meaning hers.

Shortly after I finished downloading my grandmother's music to her iPod, Kelsey, a new girl at my school, texted me and asked if I wanted to spend the night. We had met in math class and had hit it off immediately. Since she was new at school, Kelsey hadn't had time to meet a lot of people.

"We can just hang out at my house and watch movies," she wrote in her text. I texted back, "Let me ask." My grandmother said it was okay, so I called Kelsey and said I could come over. She seemed pretty excited and said her mom would pick me up at 6:00 p.m.

But that was at 4:00 p.m. At 5:00, I received another text. This one was from my friend Meghan who wrote, "A whole bunch of people are going to the movies, and then some girls are spending the night at Lauren's. Can you come?" Hmm…this sounded like a lot more fun. I liked Kelsey, but I didn't want to miss going out with the bigger group. I called Meghan, told her that Kelsey had invited me over, and asked if Kelsey could join us. Meghan was reluctant. She said, "Well, no one really knows her. I'm not sure we should invite someone Lauren doesn't know. This is really her deal, not mine. I think it might be kind of awkward."

"Okay, I said. I'll see if I can get out of it. I'll call you back." I was just about to text Kelsey that my grandmother had changed her mind, when Grandmother walked in and asked, "Are you getting ready to go? Do you need me to help you with anything?"

"Uh, no," I answered. "There's been a slight change of plans. Meghan just called and said a bunch of people are going to the movies and spending the night at Lauren's. Kelsey doesn't really know them, so I'm going to go with them and spend the night with Kelsey another night. I'm just going to tell Kelsey I can't come tonight."

Grandmother was silent, but I could tell by the look in her eye that she wasn't happy. She didn't get mad though, and she didn't even say I couldn't spend the night at Lauren's house. She just said, "How would you feel if you were Kelsey? I want you to think about that for a few minutes before you tell Kelsey you can't come. And oh, by the way, if you decide not to go to Kelsey's, you need to at least call her rather than text her with the disappointing news."

"And oh, by the way, if you decide not to go to Kelsey's, you need to at least call her rather than text her with the disappointing news."

The decision was mine to make. My excitement about going to the movies with Meghan and everyone else suddenly disappeared. I wasn't sure what to do, so I actually tried to imagine how I would feel if someone called and canceled after we had already made plans. Not too good, I guessed. In fact, just thinking about lying and disappointing Kelsey didn't feel too good, so I decided to spend the night with her. I called

106

Meghan and explained the situation. Surprisingly, Meghan seemed to have a new respect for my decision-making skills. I felt better about myself and realized I would have been feeling bad all night had I gone with Meghan instead. And I actually had a really good time with Kelsey.

The next day, when I was back with my grandparents, I glanced up and noticed a quote that had been cross-stitched in a frame and had hung on a wall at their house ever since I could remember. "Three things in human life are important: The first is to be kind. The second is to be kind. And the third is to be kind." The quote is by Henry James, and I had seen it a thousand times, but I realized that weekend I had actually put it to use.

Discussion/Self-Reflection Questions

1. What is courtesy? How do you define it? How important do you believe courtesy is as a character trait?

2. How do you think courtesy relates to other character traits? What other character traits impact courtesy?

3. What are little acts of courtesy? Why are they important? Can you think of a small act of courtesy that someone showed to you? How did that make you feel?

4. Provide examples of times you have been courteous to others. Did you find this to be natural behavior, or did you need to really think about it?

5. Do you believe that courtesy is valued in our society? How is courtesy valued in your own family? In your school?

6. Who is responsible for teaching courtesy? Who has taught you to be courteous?

7. An unknown source once said, "No one is too big to be courteous, but some are too little." What do you think it means to be too little?

8. The chapter begins with this quote from Emily Post: "Manners are a sensitive awareness of the feelings of others. If you have that awareness, you have good manners, no matter what fork you use." What does this mean to you? Do you think there is a difference between manners and courtesy? Explain.

Journaling Activity

The chapter begins with an Emily Post quote that indicates that showing courtesy is more important than using the right fork. Beyond which fork to use, create a poster for your school cafeteria that lists the top ten table manners.

It is known as a common courtesy to respond when invited to a party. Let's say you are hosting a party and have not heard from some of people you invited. As the party host, how does that make you feel? What do you do?

You are asked a question you really don't want to answer. (Maybe: What grade did you get on the history test? How much did that sweater cost? Do you want to go out with him/her?) Write a courteous response. Write a not-so-courteous response.

Today's technology demands new courtesies. Create cell phone rules for your home, your school, and your community.

This section of the book begins with the Max Erhmann poem "Desiderata." How does this poem relate to courtesy?

Chapter 14

"You must first trust in yourself before
you can trust others."

– *Anonymous*

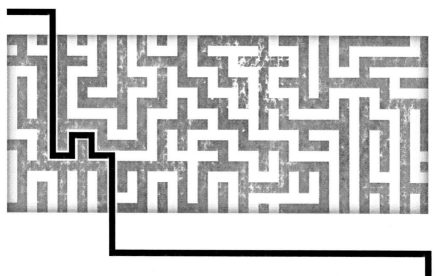

TRUSTWORTHINESS

Tied Up in Knots

I'll be the first to admit that I do not enjoy doing things that are out of my comfort zone, but when I started high school, I was forced to do so. My high school started in seventh grade, but I came in new as a new student in ninth grade. I was in a completely new world and was surrounded by 200 kids in my class who were, on that first day, mostly strangers. It was overwhelming. Not just new kids, but new teachers, and a new school that I didn't know my way around. I had no idea how to fit in.

I knew one girl a little bit because our parents were friendly and she went to my church, so after a few weeks, I started hanging out with her. She introduced me to her friends who were all pretty popular throughout the grade and the school. They hung out together all the time and were well-liked. They always seemed to be having fun and had some sort of sleepover almost every weekend.

Finally, I could breathe a little easier. I was starting to relax because I had kind of found a group, but as the year went on, I still had only one foot in the door. The girls were usually nice to me in school, but I only occasionally got invited to out-of-school activities and parties. My friends at other schools kept telling me to give it some time and that I would be invited to more stuff as they got to know me better.

Later, I started to notice that when I hung out with my new friends, all they ever did was gossip. I didn't really pay attention at first – I was too worried about fitting in and whether or not they liked me – but then I realized that they gossiped a lot and talked about pretty much everyone. One-on-one, they were all really nice, but when they got together, whoever wasn't there was at risk of being torn to pieces. Yet when we got back to school, they would smile and be really nice to the girl they had been talking about as if nothing were wrong. They would say awful things behind her back and then be sweet to her face. After watching this happen over and over, I began to question the group and myself. What was it about all of us being together that made them be so mean? And, why were they so much nicer when we were together one-on-one? I didn't know.

But I did know that I didn't want them talking about me when I wasn't around, so I was constantly watching what I said and how I acted, which started to really stress me out. I was pretty torn. I really liked hanging out with these girls and wanted badly to belong to one group, but I wasn't sure if this was how I wanted to spend the rest of high school. It was exhausting. I didn't want to be second-guessing myself all the time and constantly walking around with a pit in the bottom of my stomach. I didn't know what to do. When they started badmouthing someone, I didn't want to join in. Not only was it wrong, but I was new and had no place saying anything about anyone. I usually got very quiet when the gossiping began. I did not want to say something that I would regret, and I was uncomfortable just listening to the conversation, but if I didn't say anything, they seemed to not want me around.

One day, I was walking in the hall with my friend Holly. She and I were talking, and Michelle, a girl from the group I've been describing, walked up. She said hello to me and barely spoke to Holly. Then Michelle asked me what I was doing over the weekend and whether I wanted to come to her house. The whole time Holly was standing there saying nothing – looking awkward. I'm sure she didn't know whether to walk away, stay, talk, or keep quiet. I didn't know the answer, but I knew the feeling. And, I stood there and let it happen.

When the bell rang and we all left for class, I felt horrible, and that feeling lasted the rest of the day. I eventually realized that even though being part of a group was fun and most of the girls were nice to me when we weren't with the group, I didn't like the dynamics. You never knew who was in and who was out – who was invited to something and who wasn't. It was like a constant guessing game. I didn't need the extra stress of always questioning my friends. With your friends, you shouldn't be tied up in knots; you should be able to let down your guard. So, I decided to stop making an effort to be part of the group. I decided to do my own thing. I still liked all of the girls in the group, and they were all still nice to me when I saw them, but I just stopped caring so much about whether they invited me to do things outside of school. And when I didn't have to try so hard to be included, I stopped feeling exhausted all the time.

Soon I met some other girls and a couple of guys who were all nice

"With your friends, you shouldn't be tied up in knots; you should be able to let down your guard."

113

and fun to be around. I am really good friends with some of them today. In retrospect, I realize I was not a very confident person at that time in my life. I wasn't very competitive, and I didn't want to fight my way to the top of the social ladder. I still don't, but back then, the backstabbing made me feel a little lost. Maybe all freshmen feel that way; I don't know. I'm just thankful that I was able to break away and be independent even though I had no idea I had it in me. I guess for me, the alternative was worse.

When I look back on those four years of high school, it is amazing how much changed. The group of girls that I tried to join did not stay close friends. All of the underlying tension, gossip, and competition caused problems between them. You have to be able to trust your friends and confide in them. Status means nothing, but relationships mean everything.

Discussion/Self-Reflection Questions

1. What does trustworthiness mean to you? How important is trust-worthiness as a character trait?

2. Chandler writes that she doesn't enjoy doing things that are out of her comfort zone. What do you think that means? How about you; do you enjoy doing things outside your comfort zone? Why/Why not?

3. Has there been a time or situation when you felt out of your comfort zone? How did you deal with it? Explain.

4. How do you know if someone is trustworthy or not? What are the signs?

5. Have you ever had to end a relationship because there was a lack of trust? Was it difficult or easy? Explain.

6. It took a lot of courage for Chandler to end the friendship with the girls she didn't trust. What other character traits does it take to do what she did? What other character traits does one need to be trustworthy?

7. Has there been a situation in your own life in which you broke someone's trust? Explain. Was there something you wish you had done differently?

8. Has there ever been a time when someone you know broke his or her trust with you? How did that feel? What impact did it have on you?

9. How do you create trust?

10. The chapter begins with this anonymous quote: You must first trust in yourself before you can trust others. What do think this means? Do you agree or disagree? Can you relate that quote to Chandler's experience?

Journaling Activity

As you drive around, you might notice that there seems to be bumper sticker for every cause. What would your bumper sticker read if it were about trustworthiness?

Some of the best stories of trustworthiness can be found in children's literature. Think about the stories you have read or those that were read to you as a young child. Go online or to a bookstore or library and find a childhood picture book about trust. Relate the story to your age group – and your life today.

Trust impacts individuals and groups. Think about a sports team at your school or in your community. Describe the different aspects of trust… among coaches and players, among coaches and parents, among teammates, among coaches, and even among the parents. How can trustworthiness impact the outcome of a team effort?

Is it possible to create trusting relationships that are not face-to-face? How do you believe today's political leaders, for example, can demonstrate their trustworthiness?

Do you believe lost trust can be regained? Write about a time you lost somebody's trust or somebody lost your trust. What did you learn?

Chapter 15

"A family is only as strong as its
commitment to togetherness."

– Wes Fessler

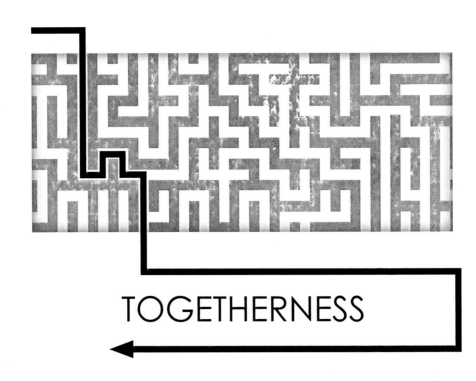

TOGETHERNESS

The Ties That Bind

Shortly before birth, I picked my family well. It was the first good decision of my new life – just kidding. We all know you don't pick your blood relatives. That is the luck of the draw. And while my parents and brother drive me crazy on many days, I have to admit that I am pretty fortunate that I wound up with them.

My mom is from Atlanta, where we live now, and my dad is from Arkansas, where we spent the first seven years of my life. Both of my parents have a tight group of brothers, sisters, and cousins who support us daily. I love going to Arkansas and spending time with my Uncle Bob, Aunt Debbie, and Cousin Marissa or taking a trip to my dad's small hometown where his second and third cousins tell old family stories. I also try to visit with my mom's family as much as I can.

But it wasn't always that way. There was a short period during my early teen years when I had a less-is-more philosophy about spending time with my family. I only adopted my current attitude after my Great-grand Aunt Jenny's ninetieth birthday.

She has since passed away, but for many years, she was the matriarch of our family on my mom's side. On her ninetieth birthday, there was a big party at our house. My mom had decided to document the occasion by making a music video that she could distribute to the whole family after the event. She moved throughout the house for the most of the evening, video camera in hand, interviewing family members, and then grabbing the digital camera to snap still shots.

My great-grandmother (Jessie, who was also Jenny's sister) passed away before I was born; but, Aunt Jenny's two children, Susie and Jason were there along with Jessie's two kids, Mary (my grandmother) and Ruth. The six of them were all very close, because in the early 1940s, when Jenny and Jessie both lost their husbands (one in an accident; the other in World War II), the two sisters decided to move in together and raise all four children under one roof.

I knew all this history, but the night of my aunt's party, their stories came alive. As we were sitting in our den, Jason shouted, "Hey, Mary, do you remember that night I dropped the flowerpot on your head while Mother and Jessie were out?"

My grandmother, who has the greatest sense of humor of anyone I know and who laughs harder at a joke than anyone I've ever seen, started to double over. "Yes," she giggled, "it's amazing you didn't kill me."

I looked over at my brother whose eyes were popping out his head. "You did what?" he asked Jason.

"Well, your grandmother would do anything I told her to when she was little," began Jason. "She was the youngest and followed us around. We were home alone one night and decided to play cops and robbers. I had been at the movies earlier in the week and had seen a getaway scene where the good guy dropped something off a building onto the bad guy's head to stop him. Naturally, as the only boy in the group, I wanted to try it, so I said, 'Mary, run around the house so I can drop this on your head from the window upstairs.' And she said, 'Will it hurt?' 'No,' I said, 'because I'm going to put it in a paper bag, and that will protect you.' So Mary ran around the front of the house and stood beneath the upstairs window, and I dropped the heavy ceramic flowerpot filled with dirt on her head, just like they did in the movies. It stopped her all right, stopped her cold." A frantic call to my great-grandmother and great-grand aunt followed because my grandmother had a big knot on her head and wouldn't stop crying.

I looked over at my grandmother and saw she was laughing so hard at the memory that tears were streaming down her face. And while the story was funny, watching her crack up made me howl louder too. Soon, everyone in the room was laughing until we cried as our relatives told more stories, like one about Ruth chasing Mary with a butcher knife, or Susie getting her hair stuck in the washing machine, or when Mary and Susie almost burned down the kitchen after trying to heat up food for their dolls. They also remembered how poor they were but how much fun they had had hanging out and being together.

When everyone left that night, I was exhausted, but it was that good, completely filled-up kind of exhaustion that comes when you've laughed and joked and told stories until you can't tell anymore.

After my mom turned out the lights downstairs, she stopped by my room, video camera in hand, and said, "I'm going to take this to the office tomorrow and edit it. Why don't you come with me and study for your test while I work on this?"

At her office the next morning, I studied in one room while my mom sat in the editing suite and worked on the video. After a few hours, she called me into the suite and said, "Watch this and tell me what you think." As the song played and I watched the video, I realized that my family was made up of a quirky group of people who were funny, crazy, strong, independent, and unconventional. They were my history. And there was something very comforting about being a part of this group – something more powerful and more satisfying than being part of any other. With family, I didn't have to do anything to belong. It was my birthright. Lucky me.

> "I realized that my family was made up of a quirky group of people who were funny, crazy, strong, independent, and unconventional. They were my history."

Discussion/Self-Reflection Questions

1. What is togetherness? How do you define it? How important do you believe togetherness is as a character trait?

2. Does togetherness require physical proximity? Do you think people can feel togetherness even if there is physical distance? Explain.

3. What other character traits impact togetherness? In order to have togetherness, what other character traits might one possess?

4. How do rituals and shared experiences impact togetherness? What are some rituals in your school? In your family? In your community?

5. What is the meaning of the term extended family? How does that relate to the concept of togetherness?

6. There are all kinds of families in the world. Do you think you have to be related by blood to be part of a family? Describe some nontraditional families you know and how they have formed a bond through spending time together.

7. Is togetherness an important element in teamwork? How does togetherness impact a sports team? A group working on a school project? The cast of a play?

8. The chapter begins with this quote from Wes Fessler: A family is only as strong as its commitment to togetherness. What does this quote mean to you? Do you agree?

9. What can be accomplished when people work together? Provide examples in your family, your school, and your community.

10. In what situation or place do you feel the strongest sense of togetherness?

Journaling Activity

Find photos or create a drawing to symbolize togetherness.

Kahlil Gibran wrote, "Let there be spaces in your togetherness." What does this mean to you? Do you think togetherness impacts individuality?

Describe an activity that you would start at your school, in your family, or in your community that would promote togetherness?

Thousands of songs have been written about togetherness. Find the lyrics to one of these songs and write about what they mean to you.

Chapter 16

"The willingness to accept responsibility for
one's own life is the source from which
self-respect springs."

– Joan Didion

RESPONSIBILITY

No Free Rides

By my junior year in high school, most of us were all driving. That meant freedom to go where we wanted. And on most weekends – someone was having a party.

My mom always told me that if she found out I had been drinking or doing drugs, she would quit her job and handcuff herself to me for a year or until she was certain that substance abuse was a road down which I wouldn't travel. It was a running joke since humor had always been a big part of my family's make-up, but I also knew that on some level, she was very serious, and if I crossed the line, the consequences from my dad and her would be pretty severe. I mean my mother was speaking at schools across the city on the dangers of underage drinking and unsupervised parties. Getting caught in either one of those situations would have been bad not just for me but for my family, because my parents' business involved helping kids make good decisions.

So on Thursdays and Fridays, when everyone was talking about who was doing what on the weekend, I had to evaluate the risks. Most of my close friends were not partiers, and we generally planned other activities – movies at someone's house, dinner, or some other way to hang out – but we weren't saints either, and when big parties rolled around because someone's parents were out of town…well, we wanted to be there as much as everyone else.

On one particular night, Tom, a guy in my class, was having a full-scale blow-out. Everybody was talking about it in school on Friday. His parents were out of the country – a pretty nice set up. Everyone I knew was going and I decided that going with them was a risk I was willing to take. My parents were actually out of town for the weekend as well, and my grandmother was staying with my brother and me. I wasn't planning on drinking and even said I would be the designated driver, but I definitely wanted to go, so I did.

At around 6 p.m., I picked up my four friends—Diane and three others—at their houses. Each ran out to my car with a bag packed. We had all planned to spend the night at Diane's after the party because she lived in the biggest house, and we could slip in the basement without having to talk to a parent when we came home. Quietly sneaking in wasn't going to be a problem for me, but everyone else who planned on drinking needed to get inside the house without getting caught, and of course, if one person got caught, we all did.

We were pretty hyped up. I cranked the music on my CD player, and everyone was singing at the top of their lungs. We stopped at a convenience store to pick up some mixers and cups, and then the vodka started flowing – out of the bags and into the cups. The drinking had started. I was nervous but not so much that I wasn't having fun. In fact, we were having a blast. Everyone was dancing in their seats, looking at the other cars, making fun of the people on the street, and laughing like crazy as we drove down the road. We were definitely in a partying mood.

When we got there, I parked my car, and we all got out, dressed in our cutest outfits. Tom had told us to park on a back street so neighbors wouldn't know how many people were there, but to get into the house from the back, we had to climb a fence and feel our way through a wet, dark wooded area and sneak across the back lawn. I'm not sure why we thought neighbors wouldn't notice a bunch of kids climbing a fence, but it was something we didn't consider. My friend Jamie tripped on a branch and landed face-first in the dirt. With mud all over her face and in her hair, Jamie did not think this was funny, but the rest of us could not keep from laughing. It was hilarious. Despite the obstacle course to get to the house, we finally made it.

Inside, the house smelled like beer and pot. Weird techno music was blaring, and I thought maybe we had just walked into the wrong party. Guys were carrying around twelve-packs, and girls were dancing and stumbling around drunk. Some were actually loaded, and others were just faking it. Since I wasn't drinking, it didn't take long for me to get bored with the whole thing. And I was starting to realize that this could get out of hand pretty quickly. If you have ever been to a party where kids are drinking and you're not, you know how miserable it can be. Kids were getting wasted playing beer pong and other drinking games, and pretty soon I felt sorry for Tom because his house was getting totally trashed, and he was going to have to clean up. All the time we were there, more kids kept showing up. I think somebody had sent a text to half the kids in the city because people from everywhere started to flow through the door. It was a steady stream of kids I knew and didn't know

127

from schools all over town. Finally, Tom freaked. He yelled across the back lawn that nobody else was allowed in, and he locked door. Not a great strategy because it ticked off the people who had driven over and climbed the fence.

The next thing I heard was that one of them had called the cops. Tom turned off the music, jumped on the coffee table, and screamed at everyone to get out of his house because the cops were coming. Widespread panic took over the room.

In a matter of seconds, everything turned to chaos. Everyone grabbed their beer and whatever else they could get their hands on and started running. People were sprinting to their cars and hopping fences. Looking back, I wish I had gotten all of this on camera because it was so insane. Literally, over a hundred kids were running all over the place. No exaggeration. Beer, vodka, and mixers spilled everywhere. The house was a total disaster. I was outside, trying to find all of my friends to tell them to get back to the car. Jenny, the spacey girl in our group, came running up to me out of breath gasping, "I can't find my purse! I think I left it in the house!"

"Are you kidding me?" I asked. "We've got to get out of here. Hurry! Go! Run as fast as you can!"

She was freaking out. She said she had to go back and get it because she was afraid if the cops did come, they'd find her wallet, pull out her ID, and end up calling her parents, so I waited for her. When I got to my car, the rest of my friends were there. They were jumping up and down and yelling for us to hurry. I started the car and sped away – no cops in sight.

You might think we would be ready to go home, but everyone wanted to stay out. It's amazing how drinking makes everything seem less dangerous than it really is. We had just run like crazy to get out before the cops came to someone's house, and now everyone was laughing and texting to find another place to take the party, so we met up in the parking lot of a nearby shopping center. We tried to regroup and figure out where to go next, but nobody could agree on anything, so we ended up just sitting there for a couple of hours, talking, listening to music, and laughing about what had just happened – telling the same stories over and over again.

As we sat in my car, I realized something: There are no free rides in life. You can't have freedom without responsibility. I told myself that being the designated driver cleared me of any wrongdoing, that since I wasn't actually drinking, I didn't bear any responsibility for what had happened that night, but I was wrong. I had four drunk people in my car, and I was responsible for their lives. I was at the party, and as a participant, drunk or not, I was part of the problem and shared the blame. What if more things had gone wrong. What if

> "There are no free rides in life. You can't have freedom without responsibility."

there had been a huge fight? What if a drunk person had stumbled and knocked over a candle and started a fire? What if the cops had come and found someone's pot? I would have been part of it all. After coming to that realization, I felt a little better about myself. Up until that point, I'd been a little uneasy – not sure what I wanted or who I was. At least now I was honest with myself and acknowledged that sometimes in life you can't play both sides.

I found out later that the police did show up at Tom's house after everyone had left. Tom and his friends took the heat. His parents were contacted, schools found out, and other parents got involved. No free rides.

Discussion/Self-Reflection Questions

1. Define the character trait responsibility in your own words. How important do you believe responsibility is as a character trait?

2. Chandler says that after being at the party, "I was starting to realize that this could get out of hand pretty quickly." What would you have done at that point?

3. Throughout life, we're often reminded to learn from our experiences. What do you think experience has to do with responsibility? Do you think it is reasonable to expect teenagers to be responsible? Explain.

4. Chandler describes party plans gone haywire. Who in the story had the ultimate responsibility for what took place? Who exhibited irresponsible behavior? (Clue: There are many to identify!) Explain.

5. On a scale of one to ten (one being not at all, ten being extremely), how responsible do you think you are? Who or what might help you to be more responsible? How would being more responsible help you and those around you?

6. Describe the most responsible action you have taken in your life so far. How did that make you feel? Did your action change the outcome of the event for you or for others?

7. The chapter begins with the quote, "The willingness to accept responsibility for one's own life is the source from which self-respect springs." How does this quote apply to Chandler's story?

8. When word spread that the police were on their way, the kids panicked and fled the party scene. Who or what do you think is responsible for enforcing responsibility in our society?

9. What can you learn from this story? What other character traits does the chapter touch upon?

Journaling Activity

Chandler writes, "What could have been a disaster for a lot of us turned out to be a problem for only a few." Rewrite the ending of the story to change the outcome. What could have happened? What other lessons might have been learned?

Television commentator Bill Maher was quoted as saying, "We have the Bill of Rights. What we need is a Bill of Responsibilities." Review the Bill of Rights. What would you include in the Bill of Responsibilities?

Adults certainly have more responsibilities than children. Does responsible behavior automatically come with adulthood? Explain.

Chandler acknowledges that she and her friends did not get caught. How has technology changed the ways people get caught? How does this impact responsibility?

Peek into your future. What can you imagine is the biggest responsibility you will ever assume? Does that image impact any of your actions today?

Chapter 17

"Respect...is appreciation of the
separateness of the other person, of the
ways in which he or she is unique."

– Annie Gottlieb

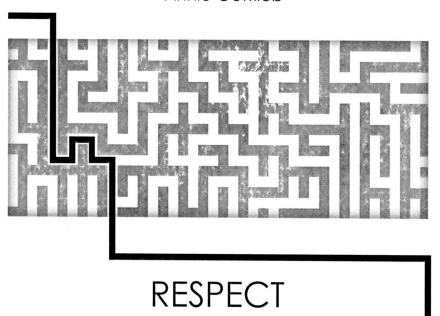

RESPECT

The Fourth "R"

Every Thanksgiving, my whole family gathers in a small town in South Georgia. My favorite part of the week is hanging out with my cousins – ten of us in all. I've always admired my older cousins, particularly two brothers, Daniel and Ben. Last Thanksgiving, Ben, the eldest, had just started his second year of teaching. Ben had talked about being a teacher ever since I could remember, wanting to follow in the footsteps of his father who had been a great teacher and coach.

But Ben's teaching career so far had not been as rewarding as he had hoped. Shortly after dinner, Ben announced that he was seriously considering giving it up. "I really thought I could make a difference in kids' lives," he said. "But it's tough. Even as an assistant coach, I don't seem to be able to get through to them. I'm frustrated in the classroom and on the field. It's just too hard to establish a connection. I don't think the kids want to have anything to do with their teachers." I was shocked. Kids need teachers like Ben. He is one of the greatest guys I know.

I told him I was actually thinking about becoming a teacher or counselor because of not one, but three teachers who had had an unbelievable influence on me. They were not traditional teachers instructing me on reading, writing, and all the other academic material. Instead, they had taught me about what has been called the fourth "R" – respect. And we had established that solid connection Ben was looking for with his students.

Mrs. Johnson, Mrs. Taylor, and Mr. Weller were teachers at my school who I came to respect more than I ever would have guessed. I met them when I became a peer leader at the beginning of my junior year. As the faculty sponsors of the peer leadership group, which was designed to help new students adjust to the school, Mrs. Johnson, Mrs. Taylor, and Mr. Weller planned activities and retreats and provided guidance, responsibilities that required them to spend countless hours away from their own family and friends. They helped put together great programs so the students could have the best possible experiences, and they went out of their way to help everyone get involved.

I've always been comfortable around adults, particularly if they're as funny, interesting, and easy-going as kids my age, so it was not a stretch for me to spend lots of hours in the peer leader office – although I'm sure some people thought it was weird that I spent so much of my free time hanging out with three teachers. Just for fun, we would take random Internet quizzes or look at funny pictures from previous retreats or school events, and I would always help out organizing events and meetings. It was during those times that I got to know Mrs. Johnson, Mrs. Taylor, and Mr. Weller as individuals, and each taught me different things.

> "I'm sure some people thought it was weird that I spent so much of my free time hanging out with three teachers."

Mrs. Johnson was quick on her feet and witty, absolutely hysterical in fact. Not only did she have a great sense of humor and the ability to make everyone around her laugh, but she was open to and accepted everyone, which was the quality I loved most about her. Students understood that they could talk to her about anything. If a seventh-grader walked into the office while I was hanging out there with a bunch of seniors, Mrs. Johnson would say hi to the seventh-grader and try to include him or her in our conversation so that the younger student wouldn't feel intimidated or awkward.

I also admired how open Mrs. Johnson was about her life. She told me some amazing stories about her time in high school and college, stories that helped me relate to her as a person rather than just as a teacher. Her openness taught me the importance of letting yourself be vulnerable and that sharing yourself, flaws and all, draws people to you. Mrs. Johnson accepted everyone for who they were and taught me that everyone is special.

Mrs. Taylor was really different but just as admirable. She always knew how to keep me in check. I had a serious problem with procrastination, but when Mrs. Taylor gave me an assignment, I knew I needed to get right on it and put 150 percent into it. I didn't want to give her anything less. She brought out my desire to work to the best of my ability. I learned more about self-discipline, hard work, and persistence from her than from anyone else.

Mrs. Taylor also encouraged me to figure out my weaknesses and work on improving them. For example, I once told her that I hated giving speeches and that I hated conflict. She told me that avoiding those activities would hold me back later in life, and she gave me practical strategies on how to approach them. She continued to work with me, finding opportunities to put those strategies into action and always encouraging me to be better.

Even though Mrs. Taylor had a strong work ethic and could be a taskmaster, she also had a softer side. Like Mrs. Johnson, Mrs. Taylor could be counted on for support and understanding. Her door was always open.

Now, I didn't know Mr. Weller as long as Mrs. Johnson and Mrs. Taylor because he came to my school later than the other two, but it didn't take me long to get to know him. Right from the start, I could sense his devotion to his students. Even though I have graduated, he stills sends emails to check in and see how things are going. He is one of the nicest and funniest guys you will ever meet. Of the three peer leader faculty sponsors, he was the one who most encouraged me to examine my inner life and spirituality. He had a sense of peacefulness about him that I strive to find in my own existence.

Mr. Weller had been all over the world and shared so much of his life experience. I admired him for using his background, intelligence, and wisdom to inspire kids. As an adult, I hope I can find the same happiness and contentment he found.

Sometimes, I know, it can be difficult to establish a student-teacher relationship like the ones I had with Mrs. Johnson, Mrs. Taylor, and Mr. Weller. There may be too many kids in the class or in the school, or a teacher may seem intimidating or hard to get to know. Ben told me that when he started to think about another career, he did some research on the teaching profession. He found a National Education Association study that reported that half of all new teachers quit the profession within five years of entering. I was surprised by that statistic and a little saddened. I thought about how different my high school experience would have been if I had not known Mrs. Johnson, Mrs. Taylor, and Mr. Weller. They had as much as or more of an impact on me than some of my closest friends. And when I think of my high school years, I will always remember them with respect.

Discussion/Self-Reflection Questions

1. How do you define respect? How important is this character trait to you?

2. What other character traits impact respect? Explain why.

3. Whom do you respect? How do you show it? How did they earn your respect?

4. Do you think you are respected by others? Explain. How does it feel to be respected?

5. What do you need to do in order to earn the respect of your parents? Your teachers? Your friends? How are those expectations different – and how are they similar?

6. What does it mean to respect yourself? Can you respect others without self-respect?

7. The chapter describes a National Education Association report about the number of teachers who leave the profession within five years of entering. What might that outcome have to do with respect?

8. It is not only people who need our respect. What else deserves respect? Why? What does respecting those other entities say about you?

9. The chapter begins with this quote from writer Annie Gottlieb: Respect...is appreciation of the separateness of the other person, of the ways in which he or she is unique. What does this mean to you? What else does this say to you about respect?

Journaling Activity

Different cultures show respect in different ways. Write about a family tradition or something in your culture that involves the concept of respect.

Abraham Lincoln, in the last line of the Gettysburg Address, stated, "… that government of the people, by the people, for the people, shall not perish from the earth." How does our government "of, by, and for the people" depend upon respect? Can we have democracy without respect?

Chandler describes the respect that she has for three special teachers. Write a letter to a person you respect. Tell him or her why you feel this way and the ways he or she impacts your life.

Statistics confirm that bullying in schools, on playgrounds, and even in the workplace is on the increase. What does bullying have to do with respect? Do you think that respect has diminished in our society?

The beginning of this book starts with the Robert Frost poem "The Road Not Taken." How does this relate to respect?

III

Inside Your World

It's Not the Critic Who Counts

It's not the critic who counts, not the man who points out how the strong man stumbled, or when the doer of deeds could have done better. The credit belongs to the man who is actually in the arena; whose face is marred by dust and sweat and blood; who strives valiantly; who errs and comes short again and again; who knows the great enthusiasms, the great devotions and spends himself in a worthy cause; who at the best, knows in the end the triumph of high achievement; and who at the worst if he fails, at least fails while daring greatly, so that his place shall never be with those cold and timid souls who know neither victory or defeat.

– Theodore Roosevelt

Chapter 18

"There is a higher court than courts of justice and that is the court of conscience. It supersedes all other courts."

– Mohandas Gandhi

JUSTICE/FAIRNESS

Wes's Last Birthday

When I agreed to work on this book over the summer after my senior year in high school, my parents gave me full access to the video library at their company. Obviously, I haven't had a compelling personal experience on every issue covered by these stories – I hate to admit that my life has not been nearly so interesting – so I sifted through tons of interviews their producers had done with kids across the country. By far, the most gripping, was the story of Rachel Davis.

Most of the stories in this book are based on true stories. I've changed names, settings, and other incidental information to protect the people involved and me. But with Rachel, I've tried to keep details as accurate as possible and have changed only the names hoping not to lose any of the impact of this story in the process. It's too important a story for you to miss anything. So while you might just skim some of the other chapters, take your time on this one.

Listening to Rachel talk about herself in high school, I realized she could have been my best friend. She was captain of the color guard, a straight-A student, and bound for college hoping to study medicine. "In high school, I didn't drink. I didn't do drugs. I just had my friends and, you know, my own little activities," she said.

"She was a kid who would play outside barefoot, go down the street knocking on doors…talking to grown-ups, playing with kids; she was a carefree, happy child." That was how her mother described her.

I knew a lot of kids like Rachel and a lot of families like hers too. In fact, from the outside looking in, almost everybody I knew was like Rachel, including me. We were good kids from solid families. While we occasionally slipped up and did the wrong thing, we didn't generally get into a lot of trouble. It's almost like we believed we were sheltered and had a layer of security that came from a stable family that protected us from our own mistakes.

But Rachel's story taught me that no one is immune. Life is not fair. The world is not always just. And, we shouldn't be so arrogant to assume that because we come from solid families, are generally pretty responsible, and make decent grades, we somehow have a free pass when it comes to bad choices.

Rachel started out doing well in college. During her first two semesters, she made the honor roll. She was going to major in biology and was thinking about medical school, but she was also having fun. She wanted to loosen up and enjoy her new independence, so she started going out a lot, drinking and partying. She bought a fake I.D. and experimented with a little pot. First it was one weekend, then another. Soon, she and her boyfriend were spending most weekends and some weeknights stoned and drunk, which is when they began to fight.

One Friday night, as usual, they went to a party, got wasted and started arguing, but this blowup was more intense than the others. Rachel ran out of the party, got into her blue Cherokee Jeep, and sped away. She didn't know where she was going really. She was just mad and hurt. Half-out of her mind, she was swerving and speeding down a dark road in the pouring rain.

Not far away, a cab driver, Wes, was making his last run of the night. He was headed home to celebrate his 51st birthday with his family as soon as he dropped off three passengers in the back seat. Wes's daughter Kendra, his wife Charlene, and his granddaughter were waiting for him. His wife said the last thing he heard before going out to work was his granddaughter telling him how much she loved him.

In another part of the city, an emergency 911 operator was at her usual late-night shift when she got the following call:

Caller: There's a blue Jeep Cherokee, like an older model style, swerving all over the road, speeding, crazy. The driver is definitely drunk, and I have a feeling he's about to run into somebody, because there's a bunch of cars up ahead. He's for sure, for sure drunk.

Operator: How long have you been behind him?

Caller: Whoa, he's about to crash. He's pretty much…He just crashed. There's a real, real bad wreck.

Operator: Tell me what he hit, sir.

Caller: He hit a taxicab. This person's definitely hurt, because their head went through the windshield, in this blue Cherokee.

Operator: Okay. Is he conscious?

Witness: They're breathing, but they're not moving. I mean, you can tell that they're breathing, but they're not moving. I

143

mean, it's real…real…for-real bad."

The caller assumed the driver of the Cherokee was a man, but it wasn't; it was Rachel Davis. In a split second, Rachel's bad choice had collided with Wes's life. She had crashed her blue Cherokee into his cab that night, killing him and seriously injuring the three passengers he was transporting.

Rachel described the moments after the accident. "I couldn't open my eyes when I was coming around. I was lying on the ground. They had just pulled me out, and I heard them say 'Oh, he's dead.' It felt like a bad dream, 'cause I was still drunk, you know. I was still pretty drunk. I said, 'Is he okay?' And they said, 'No, ma'am, there's a man that's dead.'"

Wes was dead on the scene before the medics could get him out of the car and into the ambulance. His daughter, Kendra, described him as "a quiet, caring, considerate man." His wife said, "He was a person that really liked to laugh…and that night I felt like something had been ripped apart inside of me. It was half of me that was left."

The story of the car wreck was covered in the newspaper and on television the next day. They reported that Rachel's blood alcohol level was .27, more than three times the legal limit. Because of the trauma of the crash and because she was drunk, she says she can't remember very much about that night. A doctor who had been interviewed as part of the story said, "It's like being under general anesthesia. The conscious, rational part of your brain gets put to sleep. That's what alcohol does to the brain. And you might drive a car, you might have a terrible car wreck, and, you know, you might even kill somebody and have no recollection of it the next day."

After the accident, Rachel went to court and was convicted of vehicular homicide. In other words, she killed someone with her car, and it was her fault. She was sentenced to three years in prison plus seven years probation.

"I live in a cell that's 8 feet by 11. I belong to the state," she said quietly, looking down. "The state decides that I don't have any privacy, and I have to live with that…it's because of what I did, and I can't be mad because I did it to myself. It didn't happen to me; I let it happen. And you decide yourself if you're going to let it happen to you."

I felt sorry for Rachel. Because I could identify with her, I found myself thinking, She didn't intend for this to happen. It could have happened to a lot of people. She looked and acted like so many of my friends – like me. But those feelings changed when I saw Wes's daughter, who was the same age as Rachel. She wasn't compassionate; she was angry. "I depended on my dad for lots of things. He was a major part of my life. I always thought he was going to be there for me, and now he's not. I am angry at her, and I am angry at her actions because she didn't have to make that decision at all…to drink and drive."

Kendra said it will take a long time for her to forgive Rachel, and she may never get over the hurt of losing her dad in a way that could have been prevented. It wasn't heart disease or cancer or old age; it was one huge terrible mistake that could have been avoided. "She took my father away. She still has her father. I have to go visit my father in the graveyard." She paused for a moment, and then said, "My father won't walk me down the aisle when I get married. He won't be there. She took something very important from me…and I can't ever get it back."

Not only was Rachel not immune or protected from the consequences of her bad choices, she was responsible. And her punishment was just. Three years in jail is nothing compared to the loss of a lifetime. I realized that when I heard Kendra's interview. And Rachel had realized it too. Sobbing, Rachel said, "Knowing what I have taken from them, oh my gosh…she didn't deserve that…he didn't deserve that. I am sure he wanted to watch his granddaughter grow up. I'm sure he wanted to see his daughter grow older, you know. He was the same age as my dad. And so I have a lot of guilt about what I have taken from them."

As teenagers, we think we are invincible – that somehow we can flirt with danger, make a really stupid, split-second decision, and still escape the tragic possibilities. Or worse, we don't think at all. We just react to circumstances, and like a child, we believe nothing bad will happen to us. That's what Rachel did that night. She reacted to a fight with her boyfriend. She wasn't thinking that she might kill somebody or that it was stupid to get in a car stoned and drunk. She assumed it would all turn out okay – because it always had before.

Rachel had grown up in a comfortable home in a nice neighborhood. She didn't know anyone in jail, and her parents probably didn't either. And it didn't occur to her that she might be a felon one day. "I thought it was an accident. For the longest time, I thought it was just an accident. I hid behind that for a very long time because I didn't want to admit that I may have a problem drinking," she said. "You know, I didn't want to give up this fun life I thought I was living by facing who I was…who I really was. I am part of the worst of society. Homicide…you know. I am on someone's chart or someone's list. I am labeled as one of the worst that society has to offer because I'm in prison. And that's hard to swallow, too, because I think I am a good person, you know. I am not supposed to be a felon." Her voice shook as she spoke, like she was trying her best not to cry. "I didn't think I'd ever be one of those people…you know…that drinks and drives and hurts people. But I am."

> "As teenagers, we think we are invincible – that somehow we can flirt with danger, make a really stupid, split-second decision, and still escape the tragic possibilities. Or worse, we don't think at all."

Discussion/Self-Reflection Questions

1. The character traits explored in this chapter are justice and fairness. How are those traits similar? How are they different?

2. How do you think Rachel's story and the accident relate to the concept of justice and fairness?

3. How do we determine what is just or fair? Is three years in jail a fair trade for someone's life? Explain.

4. Which person in the story experienced the greatest injustice? Wes? His family? Rachel? Her family?

5. Did Rachel get what she deserved – was justice served? Explain. Do you believe Rachel's punishment will ever cease?

6. Do you believe that Wes's family experienced a sense of fairness after the verdict?

7. The chapter begins with a quote from Mohandas Gandhi. Who was Mohandas Gandhi? Which of his actions reflected his beliefs in justice and fairness?

8. Gandhi wrote: "There is a higher court than courts of justice and that is the court of conscience. It supersedes all other courts." What does that quote mean to you? What do you think Rachel would have to say about that quote?

9. All situations of justice and fairness are not as drastic as the outcome of Rachel's accident. Describe an experience in which you witnessed or experienced justice. Can you recall an incident resulting in an injustice or unfair treatment? Explain.

10. Can people disagree on the fairness of something? Provide an example that illustrates this argument. Can people disagree on the justice of something? If people disagree, how should it be handled?

Journaling Activity

Imagine that you can look into a crystal ball. Twenty years have passed since the night of the fatal car accident. Write about Rachel's life in the future.

Young children are often heard complaining to their parents, "It's not fair!" How has your sense of fairness developed now that you are older? How do you think it will continue to develop into adulthood?

Think of people – in local or national politics, in your community, in your school – who are working for social justice. What are they doing? In what ways could you get involved?

You have the opportunity to correct any injustice you see in the world, but you have to pick one. What injustice would you correct? Why?

You have been challenged to create a "How to Be a Fair Person" poster. The first line is: Treat others the way you want to be treated. What other advice would you add to the poster?

Chapter 19

"While we are free to choose our actions,
we are not free to choose the
consequences of our actions."

– Stephen Covey

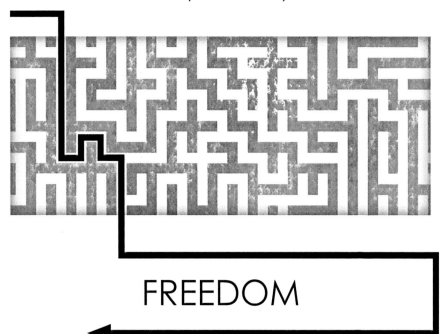

FREEDOM

Too Much, Too Soon

By the time I got to ninth grade, I had the itch. And each year it got worse. I wanted my independence – my freedom. I wanted freedom from my mom and dad breathing down my neck about where I was going, who I was going to be with, and when I would be home. I was constantly thinking, Please just back off and leave me alone. They were reluctant, to say the least, but looking back, I realize now that they did loosen their hold a little bit each year. By the summer after my senior year, they had let up considerably. And I realized, after watching a video about Derek Cordova, that for some kids, too much freedom too early comes at a great cost.

It was a Tuesday morning, and I was back at work researching kids' stories and hoping to find something that was interesting and made sense for this book. With my first cup of coffee in hand, I walked into the editing suite and powered up the playback deck. I sat down next to a high stack of videotapes, a reminder of the long workday ahead.

I picked up Tape #1 – Derek Cordova and inserted it into the play deck. I was surprised by the scene that popped on the screen. Here was a kid who looked about my age, maybe a year or two younger, getting high. That's right; it looked like he was videotaping himself in his bedroom, smoking pot, getting more stoned by the minute, and laughing and talking to the camera while he did it. I couldn't believe it, so I stopped the tape and walked into the hallway.

"Hey Jack," I called to the producer down the hall. "I'm in Edit 1 and just watched a kid getting stoned on camera. Do you know what this story is about?"

Jack walked out of his office and down the hall towards me. He was my favorite producer. Even though he was my parents' age, he was a lot cooler. Jack always wore jeans, bucks, and a wrinkled button-down shirt. He looked about 20 years younger than my parents and acted like it too. "Yeah," he said. "I interviewed that kid a few days ago. He's in rehab now, but I couldn't believe it when he told me he used to video-tape himself getting high in his own house. Then he pulled the tape out his drawer in his room and actually gave it to me. It's a crazy story – and pretty sad."

"Did he live with his parents?" I asked.

"Yeah," said Jack. "Most nights his mom was in a room down the hall. She knew he was getting high but didn't do anything about it.

"You've got to be kidding me!" I shouted.

"It's true," Jack said, and he began to tell me the full story.

Jack had interviewed Derek and his mom, Laura. According to Jack, Laura was a quiet woman with a passive personality. During the interview, she said that when Derek was about 13 or 14, she found out that he had tried drinking and then smoking pot. Her reaction? She just didn't want to deal with it. She said she thought that if she asked him about it, he would just deny it and do it anyway, so she decided to do nothing – to just ignore it – and give him the freedom to drink and get high whenever and wherever he wanted.

She told Jack that she regrets it today. In fact, Jack said she cried all throughout the interview. And as much as he liked the independence and freedom back then, Derek wishes now that someone had kept a little tighter rein on him when he was a kid.

"He had no idea what he was getting into – couldn't possibly have known how much danger he was in. And, his mom decided to look the other way, to let him find out the hard way," Jack said.

At the time of the interview, Derek was 19. He had been in out of drug treatment centers and spent a little time in jail. Jack reported, like a lot of addicts, Derek still fights the urge to use drugs and alcohol every day. Derek will be considered a recovering addict the rest of his life. He paid a high price for having freedom – too much freedom – too young.

I walked back into the editing suite, hit the play button on the deck, and finished watching the interviews, but since Jack had told me the outcome, I found myself contemplating my own life. My parents made me crazy on most days, asking too many questions and setting too many rules. It was annoying and frustrating. But maybe the alternative was worse.

"He had no idea what he was getting into – couldn't possibly have known how much danger he was in. And, his mom decided to look the other way, to let him find out the hard way."

Discussion/Self-Reflection Questions

1. What is freedom? How do you define it?

2. How important is freedom as a character trait? What other character traits might influence or have an impact on freedom?

3. Chandler writes about her teen frustration with the limits set by her parents. Can you relate to this situation? What advice would you give to Chandler?

4. What do you think about Derek's behavior? What do you think of Laura's behavior? What would you have done differently if you had been Derek's mom?

5. Who or what limits your freedom? How does that make you feel?

6. Do you believe that adults have all of the freedom? What limits or constraints are placed on adult behavior? Why?

7. Describe the freedoms that are granted to the students in your school. What happens when those freedoms are abused? How does that make you feel?

8. Describe the freedoms that are granted to the children in your family. What happens in your family when those freedoms are abused? How does that make you feel?

9. American citizens enjoy many freedoms. Create a list of our freedoms. Which freedom do you value the most? Why?

10. This chapter begins with the following quote from author Stephen Covey: While we are free to choose our actions, we are not free to choose the consequences of our actions." What does that quote mean to you? What does it say about responsibility?

Journaling Activity

The U.S. Constitution has many amendments dealing with freedom. The First Amendment addresses freedom of religion, freedom of speech, freedom of the press, freedom of assembly, and freedom of petition. You have been challenged to propose the latest amendment to the Constitution. Describe your proposal: Freedom of _____.

The Magna Carta, called the Great Charter of Freedoms, was issued in the year 1215. Research what the Magna Carta says about freedoms. Which of its principles do you believe especially apply to our life in the 21st century?

The study of U.S. history documents the evolution of freedom in our country. During the Civil Rights era, Freedom Riders rode on interstate buses into the segregated southern United States to test a Supreme Court decision outlawing racial segregation. Using what you now know about that time period, imagine yourself as a Freedom Rider. Write a letter home describing your journey.

What do you view as the biggest threat to your freedom today? Why?

Author Stephen R. Covey, who is quoted at the start of this chapter, is known for writing effective habits and tips to help people control their destiny. Write seven habits or tips you would recommend to teens in order to protect their freedoms.

This section begins with the wise words of Theodore Roosevelt from "It's Not the Critic Who Counts." How does this speech excerpt relate to freedom?

Chapter 20

"The only thing that will redeem
mankind is cooperation."

– Bertrand Russell

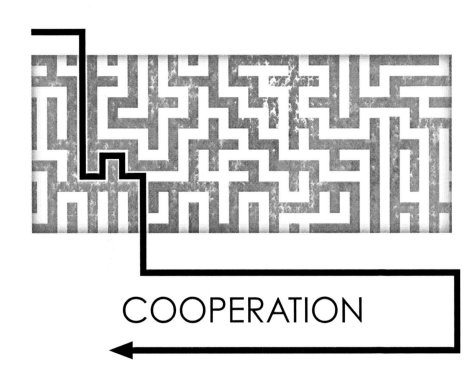

COOPERATION

Trashed

When I was a freshman, my parents took my brother and me to Washington, D.C. It was supposed to be one of those educational vacations that our parents occasionally liked to plan. Secretly, I always thought of it as "school" right in the middle of summer and wondered why I still had to be bothered with learning when I could have been at the beach. But since they were paying, we were going, and off we went to see the nation's capital. My parents thought it was important for my brother and me to visit the White House, the Lincoln Memorial, the Holocaust Museum, the Jefferson Memorial, the Smithsonian, the Capitol, and anything else we could squeeze in, so every morning we had breakfast at the crack of dawn, and headed into the city. From sunrise to sunset, we toured every historical site my parents could find on the map. I think my parents wanted the tours to leave an impression about our nation's history. Unfortunately, all around the historical sites and museums there was a ton of trash. In movies they always make those places look incredibly clean, but in person, not so much.

It was odd. Some parts of the city were really pretty and very clean. The graffiti was even like artwork. But other parts of the city seemed like garbage dumps. Dented plastic bottles, dirty Styrofoam cups, greasy fast food cardboard and paper, cigarette butts, old ripped-up newspapers, crumpled soda cans, broken beer bottles, and plastic grocery bags littered the ground. When we got close to the Potomac River, it was even worse. Everything imaginable was floating on the water, drifting toward the ocean. It was disgusting.

The trash definitely made visiting these places less enjoyable. I mean who really wants to be around a lot of trash anyway? It was weird. I was surprised that our nation's capital could be so dirty. Who ruined the river, and who dumped all that trash? Was it a few slobs or was it a million people who didn't litter much – only sometimes. I guessed it was probably the million people – everyone believing one little piece of trash wouldn't hurt. It didn't occur to me that I might be part of the million. Instead, I was just looking down on all the people who lived in the city and thinking, "How did they let it get this way?"

When I got back to our hotel room our first night, I felt gross, like I needed to take a shower. Then a random thing happened. I was channel-surfing and noticed a commercial about a program called "Not in our DC." My mom was standing right behind me and started yelling to my dad, "Hey, they're about to show our documentary on television, come watch!"

My parents had worked with the District of Columbia Department of Public Works to produce an about-to-air documentary about a group in Washington, D.C. that was trying to clean up the city. I thought, *The city definitely needs it.* But I was still ready to change the channel. We were thrilled that our parent's documentary was on television, but my brother and I really wanted to watch a movie we had picked out on pay-per-view.

Since my mom, who can get a little over-excited sometimes, was nearly hyperventilating over the fact that the program was actually on television in our hotel room, my parents wanted to forget about renting a movie and watch the documentary instead. I thought, *Oh, joy*, and my brother began to throw a fit. But it turned out okay, even though it was yet another "lesson" during a summer vacation that seemed to be full of them.

The documentary focused on kids who were passionate about litter – or getting rid of it. They had committed all their free time to cleaning up the city. One girl said, "This is where I live, and I want to be a part of the environmental effort."

And a friend of hers said, "When I see a lot of littering, I feel hurt. It's our job, the community's job, even the President's job to just keep the community clean."

The kids were all from Washington, D.C., and they seemed pretty proud that they lived in the nation's capital. I understood that, and after walking around and seeing Congress and the White House and all the memorials, I had to admit that it bothered me – as an American – that our nation's capital was so dirty.

One kid, Jackson, was in a park picking up trash with a whole bunch of other kids. Listening to him, I felt a little lazy. On the weekends and sometimes after school, he volunteered on a clean-up crew. He had been doing it for two years and started when he was 15. "Yeah, almost every week, as long as it doesn't get rained out or bad weather," he said, "we do something…clean up around neighborhoods, parks, school yards…and sometimes plant flowers or even small trees." Jackson also recruited other kids. When he had first joined the clean-up program, there were 35 kids, and by the time the documentary was produced, there were 350. He didn't sign up all of them, but a bunch of them were his friends.

"It's almost like a clean-up party," he said. He was laughing and talking and high-fiving his friends. They turned the work into a game. One guy was holding up a big plastic trash bag, and the other kids were slam-dunking pieces of paper in the bag like they were shooting hoops. Then another guy started yelling out the play-by-play, and my brother and I started laughing.

Jackson said, "You have a lot of friends when you're out here. You talk and have fun, but you're also cleaning up. You know, you're doing work, but you're also having a good time." Why was he working so hard to keep his city beautiful when on most Saturday mornings, I didn't even want to get out of bed? Maybe it was because this kid was 18 going on 80.

"We're teenagers, we're the future. We can't tell old people to do this. They've already lived their lives. They've already been here. So it's up to the younger generation…we have got to stand up together, and we've got to teach the ones that are even younger than we are. I tell them things like, 'Okay, listen…let's say you look outside your front yard and there's trash on the ground, and you know you didn't do it, but…would you just sit there and let it stay there or would you pick it up? You'd pick it up, right? It may be in your neighborhood, or it may not be in your neighborhood. But you should still do it because it's the right thing to do.'"

It sounded a little lame – kind of like a lecture from my dad, talking about right and wrong. But I had to admit he might have had a point. Picking up litter was the right thing to do. Dumping out trash was definitely the wrong thing to do. And then he said, "It will spread, you know. More of my friends will come…so it becomes a domino effect. I say to them, 'After the next few weeks, you'll think this is fun. I guarantee you.'" And I realized that was what he was saying to me.

That domino effect is the only thing that really solves a problem or any ecological issue. It's really the only way to change our environment, to be "green," or protect our planet. It's not a couple of slobs who ruin our world; it's all of us – millions, one by one, little by little – thinking that our small piece of trash or waste of energy doesn't matter. It will take all of us cooperating to turn things around. I realized then why parts of the city looked so clean and parts of D.C. were so filled with trash; this group had started cleaning up and hadn't gotten to the other part yet.

> "It's not a couple of slobs who ruin our world; it's all of us – millions, one by one, little by little – thinking that our small piece of trash or waste of energy doesn't matter."

Finally, the show was almost over. I was ready to get up and change the channel when one last girl came on the screen. She said we all needed to think about how we could help in our own cities, our own neighborhoods, and our own schools – not just in Washington, D.C. "You have to start somewhere."

Discussion/Self-Reflection Questions

1. What did the people in Washington, D.C. accomplish by cooperating and working together? Do you think the same results could have been achieved if people hadn't worked together?

2. The chapter begins with the following quote from Bertrand Russell: The only thing that will redeem mankind is cooperation. What does this mean to you? Do you agree with the statement? Why or why not?

3. What gets in the way of people cooperating sometimes? What are some ways these challenges can be overcome in order to accomplish something important?

4. On a scale of one to ten (ten being the most important), how important do you think cooperation is as a trait? Why?

5. Has there been a situation in your own life where you cooperated with others to accomplish something important? Explain. How did that feel? What were the benefits of working with others?

6. Has there been a time when you didn't cooperate with other people? Why? What happened? Is there something you wish you would have done differently?

7. Is there someone in your life who is a good example of how to cooperate with others? Describe.

8. Is cooperation learned or are some people just born cooperative? What are some ways that we can all learn to better cooperate with one another?

9. What is the difference between cooperation and compromise? Can we have one without the other?

Journaling Activity

After reading the story related to the character trait of cooperation, define the trait in your own words in the space below.

What key messages or lessons did you take away from the story about cooperation?

If you could change one thing about your school or community, what would it be? How would you get others to cooperate with you in order to implement that change?

Write about how cooperation (or lack thereof) changed the outcome of a situation you experienced...perhaps when you least expected it.

When it comes to making laws and enforcing them, cooperation is clearly a key factor. What messages do you think our government leaders send about cooperation?

Chapter 21

"Every Action done in company, ought to be with some sign of respect, to those that are Present."

– Rule No. 1 of George Washington's Rules of Civility and Decent Behavior

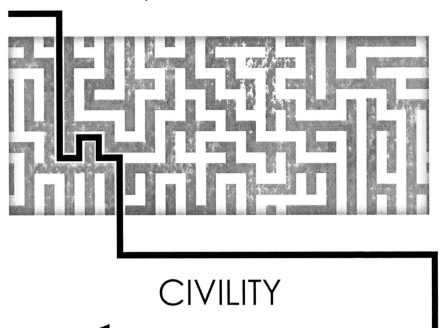

CIVILITY

Web Wars

Some people say girls are mean, at least meaner than boys. They say we gossip more, make fun of each other, and get into catfights with other girls. They say boys are more upfront with each other; if a boy does something another guy doesn't like, they will confront each other, deal with it, and then get over it so they can get back to being friends. But girls? The conventional wisdom is we talk behind each others' back, say mean and nasty things about someone especially when she's not around, and then, instead of confronting each other in an open way, we cry and think about how to get revenge.

That's what people say, but I don't think it's true. If you were to lump girls and boys together and study how all of them dealt with competition and rivalry and hurt feelings, you would probably find that girls and guys aren't all that different. Still, I know a girl named Caroline who was the victim of some mean kids, both boys and girls, but mostly girls. It started in middle school when a few girls starting spreading sexual rumors about her and calling her some nasty names.

Caroline said, "The first time I was accused of it, I was so confused because I had never been called that before. And these were strong words to be thrown at you when you're only 13. Before this, if anything, I was called a prude. It was so random. It popped up out of nowhere, and some of these girls were my best friends. At least I thought they were."

At first, Caroline said, she tried to ignore the harassment, thinking that in time, it would go away, but it didn't.

And she said, if the girls knew you were Caroline's friend, you got picked on too.

As the intimidation continued, Caroline was diagnosed with a mild case of depression. When the other kids somehow found out about that, they added it to their list of things to tease her about. When she talks about what happened, it's hard to listen and not get mad, I mean really outraged.

"I remember one day in class, I was sitting next to this boy, a guy I used to go out with. Before the teacher got there, he held up a sign that read, 'Psycho.' It was horrible. He wrote it on a piece of paper, 'P-S-Y-

C-H-O,' in big letters. And I just put my head down on my desk, and I didn't say anything. I just started crying."

Things were no better when Caroline got home from school, because everyone used the Internet to continue their attacks. It seemed as if there was a mob mentality; when a few kids got online and started saying cruel stuff, other kids picked it up, and it continued to spread. They used Facebook, email, and instant messaging to make Caroline's life miserable.

"After a while, that computer screen became the enemy," her mom said. Caroline may have cried a lot back then, but even now her mother can't talk about what those kids did to her daughter without tears welling up in her eyes. "There were times when I wanted to take a hammer and just smash that screen! I hated the power it had to get in the house and hurt her."

"It turned out to be a doorway for more violence, for more harm and aggression against her," Caroline's dad said.

Caroline added, "Even at home I wasn't safe. People could still call me. They could still contact me through the Internet or a web site or texting. I could not get away."

Why did those kids act that way? Maybe they knew they could hide behind a computer screen without Caroline knowing who it was. They could be jerks without consequences. On the Internet, there were no cops or teachers or parents or vice principals watching their every move.

> "Even at home I wasn't safe. People could still call me. They could still contact me through the Internet or a web site or texting. I could not get away."

In the end, the harassment stopped, but not because the bullies gave up. It stopped when Caroline's family moved away. They moved to a new city, and Caroline went to a new high school where the kids were nice to her. And now, she says, when she hears another kid saying something mean to someone else, she won't put up with it. "If I see it happen to other girls, I don't sit by and watch. I get involved and put an end to it."

Discussion/Self-Reflection Questions

1. How do you define civility? How important is civility as a character trait?

2. What other character traits do you think impact civility? Explain.

3. What do you think civility has to do with manners?

4. Some schools and businesses require uniforms. Many schools and businesses have dress codes. Do you believe that one's manner of dress impacts civility?

5. Who do you look to as a role model for civility?

6. Who do you believe is responsible for teaching civility?

7. How do you think today's technology has changed the rules of civility?

8. Do you think you treat others with civility? Do you believe that you are treated with civility? Provide examples.

9. John F. Kennedy once said, "So let us begin anew – remembering on both sides that civility is not a sign of weakness…" Do you believe civility might be interpreted as a sign of weakness? Explain.

Journaling Activity

This chapter begins with the first of George Washington's 110 "Rules of Civility." Create at least ten rules of civility for today.

Find a recent news story that demonstrates civility – or the lack thereof. How did others react? What is your reaction? What do you think this says about our society?

Imagine you can look into the future. Write about the society and civility you see in the 22nd century? Have people changed their ways? If so, how?

The word civilité shares the same etymology (origin) with words like civility, civilized, and civilization. The root word means to be "a member of the household." Describe the qualities of the household – at school, at home, and in your community – of which you would wish to be a member.

This section of the book begins with words from Theodore Roosevelt's speech excerpt, "It's Not the Critic Who Counts." How does this relate to civility? What does this mean to you?

Chapter 22

"The price of the democratic way of life is a grow-ing appreciation of people's differences, not merely as tolerable, but as the essence of a rich and rewarding human experience."

– Jerome Nathanson

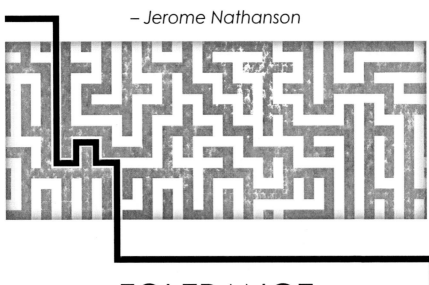

TOLERANCE

Different Skin, Same Blood

Most days, I tolerate my younger brother and my parents when they are making me crazy. But in our communities and beyond, tolerance takes on a whole new meaning.

I once heard someone say, "We need to move beyond tolerance. You can only tolerate someone for so long. After a while you need to find a way to accept and appreciate."

That person's name was Jack. His story was unlike almost any I'd ever heard. Jack is now 58, but when he was 10 and his brother was 6, his parents, Dan and Emily, bought a house in an African American neighborhood. They were white.

While it seems outdated to identify neighborhoods by race in this day and time, then it was common. That was almost fifty years ago, in the early 1960s, when racial tension was more intense than ever in our county.

Why did they move to that neighborhood? Because Dan and Emily wanted to help change race relations in America. Both had protested and marched against discrimination during the civil rights movement. Both had campaigned for the passage of the Civil Rights Act in 1964. But Jack said that his parents honestly believed that until "white people lived in the same neighborhoods with black people," nothing would really change. He said his parents wanted to see and learn and know an America that was different from the one they knew growing up, and they wanted their children to know something different as well.

Jack remembered his father telling him, "The whole idea of education is not just to get good grades and go to college, but to learn how to live in a community outside of your own. Because I don't care who you are, you are going to have to live in a world with people who are unlike yourself. To limit yourself to one type of person and one way of living, you know, that's not what life is about. The world is opening up, and we need to get to know each other."

But there was also a more personal reason they moved to the neighborhood, a deeper reason that made Emily so passionate about changing things.

When Emily had been a child, her family had an African American maid named Margie. Emily often talked to Jack about Margie, about how much she loved Margie and how Margie was such a big part of Emily's family. But one day, when she went with her mom to drive Margie home, Emily saw some things that made her very sad and left a lasting impression..

They drove back in the woods where there weren't any roads, just ruts in the mud. And as they got further back into the neighborhood where Margie and her family lived, Emily could only see broken-down shacks. Jack said he remembers seeing tears in his mother's eyes when she talked about the poverty and about how hard it was to see someone she loved so much living like that.

So when Emily grew up, got married, and had kids of her own, they moved to a neighborhood that had a total of four white faces...theirs.

Jack said, at first, the kids called him names. "I've been called cracker, wigger, just a lot of different stuff. I felt like I stood out, and I could tell when people were looking at me...staring at me."

He understood why people would stare; he and his brother were the only white kids on the block and the only white kids in their school, which was unheard of back then. "I didn't know how to make friends," Jack said. "I knew I stuck out, really badly, and I didn't want that. Nobody really wants that."

Jack remembers the pain he felt – and the days that he just didn't want to go back to school. That first year, the kids at his school invented a nickname for him – White Boy J. "Jack is where the J comes from, and the White Boy just tells who I am. I guess it's racial...but it's not really a racial slur. I was white and my name was Jack, so I was White Boy J," he recalled.

Initially, Jack liked getting a nickname because, in a way, it meant that he wasn't so strange anymore; a lot of the kids had nicknames... and he was one of them. Jack said, "At first, I just had this real need to be accepted, so I picked up that name really quickly. People called it, and that was just my thing. I was the white guy at the school, White Boy J, because there weren't any others. People would judge and interact with me on that level, using that name, but then later on, I realized this needs to change." He wanted to be one of the guys, without a label.

It was then that Jack became aware that he had experienced feelings similar to those who had been prejudged for decades based on the color of their skin. "We all want to be judged for who we are, not how we look," said Jack.

So looking back, was the move to this neighborhood good for Jack and his family during such a sensitive time in our history? "Yes," said Jack without hesitation. "Moving into that neighborhood was the only way our family could even begin to understand what African Americans and so many other minorities dealt with for generations. And it still wasn't enough. We would never completely get it. But it made me a much stronger person, and I just have such a heightened sensitivity to issues of race now. I mean…I think we're all really the same people. We just have different cultures and different backgrounds."

> "People are people, you know? We have the same color blood. We experience many of the same anxieties and emotions and dreams."

Many years have passed since Jack was a kid, but the challenges remain. His experiences at a young age, like his mom's, helped him really learn what perhaps too many of us never do: that people are people. We have the same color blood. We experience many of the same anxieties and emotions and dreams. We worry about the future and about our families. We have the same physical needs and the same need for joy, security, and love.

Maybe we can't experience that and truly appreciate each other until we live together, work together, eat together, and go to school together. Tolerance is just the first step of many in true understanding. Jack's family was right – and maybe way ahead of their time.

173

Discussion/Self-Reflection Questions

1. What does tolerance mean to you? How do you define tolerance?

2. There are many character traits reviewed in this book. How important to you is the character trait of tolerance?

3. What situations in your life have required tolerance on your part?

4. When have others exhibited tolerance – or a lack thereof – towards you? What did you learn from the experience?

5. On a scale of one to ten, one being totally intolerant, ten being extremely tolerant, how do you rate tolerance in American society today? Within your family? Within your school? Within your community? Within you?

6. What, if anything, is done to promote tolerance in your family? In your school? In your community? How might you change that?

7. The chapter describes experiences with cultural diversity that lead to acceptance. How diverse is your community?

8. The chapter begins with this quote from Jerome Nathanson: The price of the democratic way of life is a growing appreciation of people's differences, not merely as tolerable, but as the essence of a rich and rewarding human experience. What does this quote mean to you?

9. How do you think things have changed in our nation since the passage of the Civil Rights Act in 1964? Do you think kids you know are more tolerant and accepting of differences than your parents' generation? Explain.

10. This section of the book begins with Theodore Roosevelt's "It's Not the Critic Who Counts." What does this passage say about tolerance?

Journaling Activity

Eric Hoffer, an American philosopher, wrote, "The capacity for getting along with our neighbor depends to a large extent on the capacity for getting along with ourselves. The self-respecting individual will try to be as tolerant of his neighbor's shortcomings as he is of his own." What does it mean to get along with oneself? Are you tolerant of your own shortcomings? Explain.

Open a newspaper, go online, or watch the television news. Find a recent news item and describe the ways in which people exhibited tolerance – or intolerance. Write about how a different position might have changed the outcome of the news story.

Mark Twain wrote, "Travel is fatal to prejudice, bigotry, and narrow-mindedness, and many of our people need it sorely on these accounts. Broad, wholesome, charitable views of men and things cannot be acquired by vegetating in one little corner of the earth all one's lifetime." Describe a travel experience – near or far – that had an effect on your tolerance.

Let's say you are charged with creating a new EPCOT exhibit at Disney World to promote worldwide tolerance. Describe what travelers would experience there.

Chapter 23

"When the power of love overcomes the love of power, the world will know peace."

– Jimi Hendrix

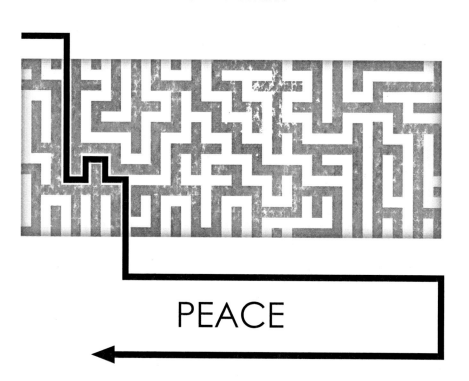

PEACE

A Random Hit

Think about this. It's Friday afternoon and you get home before anyone else. You're by yourself. It's winter and almost dark. The street is quiet. It's a free weekend. You're going out later, but for a few minutes you have some peace and quiet. You grab the remote, dive for the couch, and throw your feet up on the armrest. And then you're hit – a single, earth-shattering sound and an indescribable, unbearable pain that rips through your body. In a second you're down – on the floor – the victim of a violent attack.

That is what happened to Ronnie Greer. He was 15 and home alone when a stray bullet exploded in his back from a drive-by shooting. I found out about Ronnie while I was researching a paper on violence in America. A few days after receiving the assignment, I had stopped by my parents' office to drop something off. While I was there, I ran into their editor-in-chief who runs the production department. He was sitting in the editing suite watching the final version of a documentary, "Young Guns," about kids and violence. While I don't usually like to hang out at my parents' office, this looked like something that might work for my paper, so I decided to stay and watch.

"Man, I can't really describe it. It's..." said Ronnie Greer, "I mean it was just like getting hit with a sledgehammer. Like, man, I don't know, just struck down by lightning or something. Just crazy. It was so bad, so strong, and the hurt – I don't know how to say it."

Ronnie is now paralyzed. The bullet shattered his vertebrae. He has long black dreadlocks, strong arms, a square face, and wide-set eyes. Throughout the interview, I never saw him smile. He kept leaning forward in his chair, he said, because it hurt to lean back. "Yeah, the bullet is still in there. At the time, they couldn't remove it because it was life-threatening. They just took the bone fragments out of my back. They did the surgery, they took the bone fragments out, and they left the bullet in there," said Ronnie.

He didn't talk about the night he was shot and said he doesn't remember very much, but he did remember how it felt the moment the bullet hit him. "When I did get shot, one of the first things I saw when I opened up my eyes...was like a vision of my legs...flying. Like they had wings, and they were flying up in the air. Like honest to God," he said with tears in his eyes. "Talking about this, it's so emotional now, 'cause it's just like I can still see it. And it's crazy. I didn't know I was I was going to be in a wheelchair, but I knew my legs were no longer going to be a part of my life."

I had been researching my paper for several nights, and the statistics had started to run together. But watching Ronnie brought the numbers to life. According to the Centers for Disease Control (CDC), homicide and suicide are the second and third leading causes of death for kids our age. Unintentional injury is the only thing that kills more kids. That was a shock. I didn't personally know anyone who was affected by that kind of violence, but seeing Ronnie made it real for me.

At the end of the interview, the camera zoomed out and panned across the room. I could see Ronnie in the wide shot, sitting in a stainless steel wheelchair. No motor. He had to use his arms to move the wheels. I guess it's possible some medical breakthrough will happen someday, but most people, including Ronnie, believe he will be in that chair the rest of his life.

"You're rolling around and everybody's taller than you. So they, the world looks down on you now. You know what I'm saying? Because you don't want to admit it, but…you are inadequate in a way of being, just like being a man. I mean there's different stages to this…it runs so deep. You know…I date girls," he said. "I do date…but I can't never really get too serious about it, because I just feel like, I just feel like I'm inadequate, you know what I'm saying?"

I can tell from watching him that being paraplegic is very, very difficult and that he is still in a lot of physical and emotional pain. "Throughout the day I break down, or whatever. I have an outburst. I literally will cry, you know what I'm saying, and need some time to get myself together. Every day, that's what it is. Just the emotional turbulence. I'm never stable. I'm never feeling like 'Okay, I'm all right. I'm gonna be all right.' You're never all right."

"Whenever I hear about violence, I think about power. It seems to me that we use violence as a way to get control in a crowded and complicated society."

What makes our society so violent? The judge on Ronnie's case had some theories. "It's hard to believe, why kids shoot each other. 'I'm shooting you because you looked at my girlfriend.' That's what they'll tell you. Or...'I asked you to give me your cell phone and you won't give it to me. So I'm going to shoot you to take your cell phone.' Or... 'You crossed over into my block, and you're from another neighborhood," she said. "It's really pathetic."

Whenever I hear about violence, I think about power. It seems to me that we use violence as a way to get control in a crowded and complicated society. We want to control our friends, our neighborhoods, our enemies. We all want to live at the top. And violence is sometimes a fast, simple way to get what we want in a society that seems to accept it is as an option.

Whether you agree with that or not, one thing you have to admit is that violence is everywhere – in our music, video games, movies, on the news, in schools, and overseas. I used to roll my eyes when my parents wouldn't let my brother play violent video games. Now I'm rethinking that, because I wonder if little by little, when we live with violence and accept it as part of our daily culture, we are saying it's okay. Someday will it just become a routine part of life? Has that already happened in some parts of our country? I think so. There are some people who live with violence every day. They've come to expect it and accept it.

The credits roll, the show is over, and it's time for me to get back to my easy, peaceful life, but not Ronnie. Late one Friday afternoon, Ronnie became the victim of a random act of violence. He can't walk away from the wheelchair and can't rewind to those not-a-care-in-the world afternoons. A culture of violence changed all that. He, most likely, will never grab the remote, dive on his couch, and throw his feet up to rest peacefully again.

Discussion/Self-Reflection Questions

1. What is peace? How do you define it?

2. When do you feel most peaceful? When do you feel the least peaceful? Describe those times. What are some ways that you can increase the feeling of peace in your own life?

3. The judge in the story talks about the reasons kids shoot each other. She said sometimes it's over someone's girlfriend or someone crossing over to the wrong block. What do you think about these reasons? Why do you think kids shoot each other?

4. How do you think peace impacts the other character traits? How do the other character traits impact peace?

5. Do you think it's possible to create more peaceful communities? If so, what are some ways that we can all create a more peaceful community, school, or classroom?

6. Do you feel safe at school? In your community? What would you do if you felt threatened?

7. What are some ways that you think Ronnie could bring more peace to his life after what has happened to him?

8. The chapter begins with a quote from musician Jimi Hendrix: "When the power of love overcomes the love of power, the world will know peace." What does this statement mean to you? Can power and peace co-exist?

Journaling Activity

Jim Hendrix's quote, "When the power of love overcomes the love of power, the world will know peace," begins this chapter. Hendrix was an American guitarist, singer, and songwriter who headlined at the iconic Woodstock Festival in 1969. Go online and do a little research about America during the 1960s. How could the turbulence of that decade have influenced Hendrix's thinking?

Think about the music and lyrics you listen to. What are some of your favorite musicians saying (or singing) about peace? Provide examples.

Complete this sentence: I was most angry and frustrated when…

Did an act of violence ever enter your mind? How did you resolve the situation? What would you have done differently?

The chapter describes very real stories of gun violence. What do you think about a society without weapons? Do a little research, if necessary, and write about your thoughts on gun control.

Imagine you have been offered the opportunity to present a local version of the Nobel Peace Prize to someone in your school, family, or community. Who would you select? Why?

Chapter 24

"The only title in our democracy superior to that of President is the title of citizen."

– Justice Louis D. Brandeis

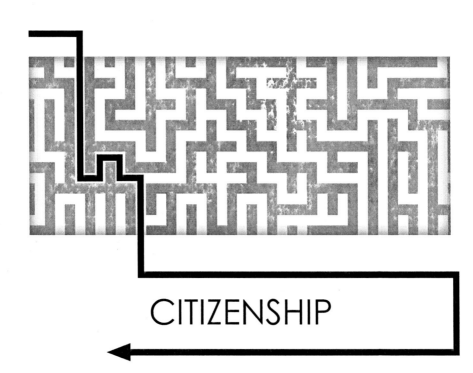

CITIZENSHIP

The Quality of Our Response

In the middle of the long nights, he could hear gunshots. Far away, somewhere out in the dark, there were tiny explosions, each one a bullet. Were they aimed at him? No. The gun, probably an AK-47, was too far away. He would lie in his cot, in the 90-degree heat, listening and hoping that the sound wouldn't get any louder.

David is a Marine who fought in the war in Iraq. His mom is one of my mom's best friends from childhood. So, our families have known each other for years. As kids, we played together in the backyard. I remember his toy guns and GI Joe games. Now I know it was more than just childhood play. He says he's always wanted to serve his country. So, at the age of seventeen, in the middle of his senior year in high school, when the rest of us were sweating out college admissions and what would come next, David headed down to the Marine recruitment office to find out how to enlist.

I never would have expected that from him. David is preppy (in his pink button-down shirts and plaid shorts, he looks more like a college fraternity guy than a military man) and talks with a Southern drawl. Apparently, I wasn't the only one who wouldn't have expected it. Neither did his parents or sister. One night, as our families had dinner together, they told us about the night David announced he wanted to put his college acceptances on hold and go to Iraq. He was only seventeen so he needed his parents' permission to enlist – and that was a problem.

His mom told us it was one of "the hardest conversations she ever had with anybody...ever," in her entire life. They talked about dying and about getting wounded or disabled. But there was nothing they could say or do to change his mind. David wanted to fight for his country. He signed the enlistment contract, convinced his parents to co-sign, and joined the Marines right after high school graduation.

Next was boot camp. And, David says he was a little unprepared for what would be the worst thirteen weeks of his life. He had to make it through training in the hot, swampy marshes of South Carolina. Every day, an unsympathetic, angry Marine drill instructor yelled at him incessantly trying to get him in shape mentally and physically. He was told he didn't have what it takes, that he would never make it out of boot camp. That he was weak – not nearly tough enough to become a Marine – and that the only way for the pain to end was to quit. Day-after-day, the drill instructor tried to break David down.

Then David described a defining moment when something changed, the moment he really understood what it meant to serve and to truly be a good citizen. "I was exhausted, mentally, physically, and emotionally. Every bit had been taken out of me that day. Then one of my drill instructors made a comment. He said my parents must have been horrible people, that '...they must have been terrible parents to raise something as worthless as you.' That hurt. I stopped what I was doing, got up, looked at him, and said... 'This recruit's faults are his own...and don't ever talk about my parents again.'"

David was scared: He was talking back to the drill instructor – correcting him, arguing with him, telling him what to do. He expected the worst kind of punishment, but the sergeant was silent, just nodded his head, and said nothing. And at that point, David realized that he had passed some kind of unwritten test. It was the kind of response they were waiting for the whole time – that when you were at your weakest point, when you had nothing left to give, the Marines wanted you to still be able to stand up for yourself, for your community, your country, and to protect the people you love.

> "We think about it mostly in terms of being a citizen of our country. But citizenship is also about that 'quality of an individual's response' to people in our family, our school, our neighborhood, and any other community of which we are a part."

The dictionary defines citizenship as "the quality of an individual's response to membership in a community." We think about it mostly in terms of being a citizen of our country. But citizenship is also about that "quality of an individual's response" to people in our family, our school, our neighborhood, and any other community of which we are a part. In his weakest moment, David was willing to take whatever the drill sergeant was capable of dishing out – no matter how bad it was – in order to protect his parents. It was the highest form of service, the highest quality of response.

I hope I could overcome that kind pressure and show that kind of loyalty and citizenship in those circumstances. But I'll never really know unless, like David, I'm put to the test. I mean...final exams or suicide drills at basketball camp or getting my wisdom teeth yanked out is as tough as it has been for me. I know nothing about thirteen weeks of exhaustion and humiliation. Would I be able to do it? Would I even want to do it?

David said the Marine Corps makes boot camp miserable so you don't crumble when you show up for the real thing. "When someone is pointing a gun at your face or hiding a bomb along the road, you can't run away and hide or try to talk it out with the enemy," he said. "You have to be willing to defend, to react, to make a split decision without hesitation and protect yourself, the other soldiers around you that have your back, and your country." He was trained well. And, thankfully, he made it home okay after an eight-month tour of duty.

When our families met for dinner, we watched a video his dad had taken at the bus station the day David had come home. You can see an amazing scene with hundreds of parents, wives, girlfriends, boyfriends, and little kids waiting for their Marine to climb out of one of the buses. They are all citizens in their own families and communities. At first everybody is standing around, talking and smiling and nervous, and then finally someone spots their soldier and the jumping, hugging, and tears start.

I guess how we respond when a Marine returns from war is a kind of citizenship, too. That "quality of our response" is a kind of service to our country and to the men and women in our community who are willing to fight for us. They deserve our highest form of respect for the sacrifice they make and the service they provide. Watching that video made me feel a little better, and a little less embarrassed that I questioned whether I would have the guts to go to war. We all have the ability to serve in our own way, to be loyal and to protect the community around us.

Discussion/Self-Reflection Questions

1. What does citizenship mean to you? How do you define it?

2. How did David show good citizenship by joining the military?

3. Why was it important for David to join the military? What did it mean to him? What did he learn through his experience?

4. Chandler says the dictionary defines citizenship as the "quality of an individual's response to membership in a community." What does that mean to you? How do you think David's parents, neighbors, and friends showed good citizenship by supporting David at home?

5. Would you be willing to put yourself in harm's way like David did to show good citizenship? Why/Why not?

6. What issues are important enough for you to stand up for what you believe, even if it may be difficult and painful?

7. Is there a time when you demonstrated good citizenship? What happened? How did it make you feel?

8. Is there a time when you wish you would have stood up for something you believed in and didn't? What happened? What would you have done differently?

9. What are some ways besides joining the military that people can demonstrate good citizenship?

Journaling Activity

Is there someone in your life who you think demonstrates good citizenship? Explain.

The United Nations Correspondents Association issues an award to a "Citizen of the World." Why does the U.N. select an individual to honor with that title? What do you think it means to be a citizen of the world?

If you had the freedom to travel to any city or country in the world, where would you go and why?

Justice Brandeis wrote: "The only title in our democracy superior to that of President is the title of citizen." What role did Justice Brandeis play in American history? What do you think he means?

And the Journey Continues...

"Promise me you'll always remember: You are braver than you believe, and stronger than you seem, and smarter than you think."

– *Christopher Robin to Winnie the Pooh (by A. A. Milne)*

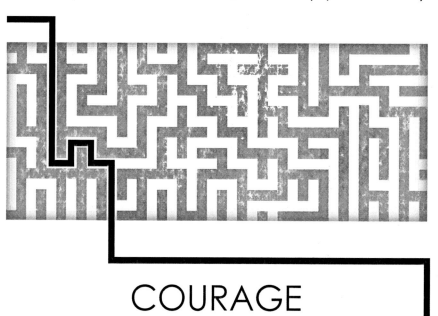

COURAGE

Facing the Future

When I first started high school, I was quiet and shy. It's not my nature now, nor was it as a kid when I would have been described as a sometimes loud, precocious tomboy – not reserved or bashful. But in my early teen years, I was unsure of myself, so I retreated into my shell. As a high school freshman, I played it safe and stayed in the background. And that reputation stuck. So at the end of my junior year, when I started applying to colleges, I decided I wanted a fresh start. I wanted to go to a school where I didn't know anyone and where I could break out of my shell. I wanted to recreate my image, and see what it felt like to go to a school where no one had any preconceived notions about me.

I decided to focus my college search on small schools in the South because I wanted to be away from home but not too far away. I was also looking for a school between 4,000 and 8,000 students because I felt like it would be easier to get to know people in a smaller environment. It was difficult to find a school that I liked, met my distance and size criteria, and would accept someone with my grades and SAT scores, but I finally did, in North Carolina. I liked it so much that I decided to apply for early decision, which meant that if I got in, I was committed to attend.

As December of my senior year approached, I waited for the news. When I found out I had been accepted early decision, I went crazy! I was jumping up and down – so excited – for about half an hour. Then reality set in. I would be attending a school I really wanted to go to, but I'd be going alone. The fear was building when the phone started ringing and Facebook statuses began changing by the second. Everyone was talking about who got into what school and how much fun they were going to have once they got there. Most kids were going to a college where they'd know at least one friend, but I was going solo. Nobody in my class had even applied to the small school I had chosen.

I started to panic; my excitement turned into anxiety. What was I thinking! I was now committed to attend. I wasn't going to know anyone. Had I been temporarily insane when I had applied there? That night my mom came into my room and said, "Why don't we take a trip to North Carolina in a couple of weeks? I just looked at your school's website, and there is an orientation coming up for kids who were accepted early decision." I thought about it and agreed to go.

Later that month, Mom and I packed up the car and drove four hours to my new school in North Carolina. We had made reservations at what was supposed to be a really cool bed-and-breakfast, but when we walked into the lobby to register, nothing but negative thoughts crowded my mind. The inn looked nice enough, but I kept thinking, This is a tiny town. It's going to be boring. Where are all the people?

At dinner that night, my mom noticed three other women about her age and what looked like their daughters at a nearby table. My mom, who will talk to a wall if given a chance, looked over, smiled, and then asked if they were in town for the weekend orientation at the university. "Yes," said one of the women, "I'm from Baltimore, and this is my daughter Emily." Another one chimed in, "And, we're from New Jersey, and this is my daughter Kayla." And then the third remarked, "We're from Virginia, and this is my daughter Ashley. Would you like to join us?"

"We'd love to," said my mother who had practically pulled up a chair before we were even invited. I was a little embarrassed and skeptical, although I had to admit all three girls looked normal and kind of like some of my friends from home. So, even though all those old feelings of insecurity came rushing back and I wanted to sit in my chair and not say a word, I forced myself to speak up. I knew that this was possibly the start of a new beginning, a time to let people see who I really was, even if that meant being uncomfortable at first.

I started talking – probably a little too much to begin with, but it was better than saying nothing at all – and pretty soon, I forgot that I was nervous and stopped thinking about myself. I was so focused on learning about Kayla, Ashley, and Emily that I completely lost myself in the moment. I had never been to Maryland, Virginia, or New Jersey, so it was fun to listen to their accents and hear about their schools. Pretty soon, we were all laughing and ignoring our mothers, who were at the other end of the table, drowning us out with their own conversation.

We sat in the restaurant for about two and a half hours, exchanged cell phone numbers, and agreed to text the next morning so we could meet on campus at the first session. I was relieved. And I was having a good time.

The weekend was a blast, and we all hung out during the daytime sessions and at the basketball game the next night. In fact, I lost my mom sometime after the on-campus dinner and didn't see her again until we went back to the hotel. I was starting to think, I'm going to like this place.

After that weekend visit, I had a new perspective and attitude. Starting college is one of the first times in your life when you can completely reinvent yourself. You are independent for the first time and only really answer to yourself. You have the opportunity to change how you are viewed, how you do in school, and what you do outside the classroom. You get to meet new people and be anyone you want.

That weekend orientation, during which I made new friends and got to learn more about my university, gave me a new kind of confidence. I knew that I wanted to make the best of this upcoming time in my life and spend the next four years at a school that would prepare me for the future. I wanted a school that would encourage me to be my best. I realized that if I were to go to a college with a bunch of my friends, I would get lost in the crowd, I would not push myself to step out of my comfort zone, and I would have trouble taking advantage of the fresh start I was about to be given.

I'm still a little nervous about what lies ahead, but I feel good that I made a decision to take a risk. I played it safe in high school, but I don't want to play it safe in life. For me, the first steps were picking a school where I knew no one, making a decision to speak up even when I wanted to sit in silence, and forgetting about my own worries so that I could learn about others and they could get to know me.

> "I played it safe in high school, but I don't want to play it safe in life."

One of my favorite sayings is "Life is a journey, not a destination." I realize that mine is just beginning. My goal is to face my fears in all situations. My hope is that this book will help you do that too.

Discussion/Self-Reflection Questions

1. How do you define courage? How important is courage as a character trait?

2. What other character traits do you think impact courage? Explain.

3. Chandler describes the courage it took for her to leave home and go off to college. What experiences have you been through that required courage? Who or what did you turn to for support?

4. What would have happened if Chandler had failed to show courage?

5. Does being courageous always involve risk-taking? Why or why not?

6. Who do you look to as a role model for courage?

7. How many ways can you complete the following sentence: It takes courage to…?

8. What recent news stories depict acts of courage? What words are used to describe the situation? What did the participants have to say?

9. Here are three words: courage, encourage, discourage. Take the words a part. What is the root word? How does the prefix change its meaning?

10. The chapter begins with this Christopher Robin quote to Winnie the Pooh in one of A. A. Milne's stories: "Promise me you'll always remember: You are braver than you believe, and stronger than you seem, and smarter than you think." What does this have to do with courage? How do you believe attitude affects courage?

Journaling Activity

Explore the differences and similarities between moral courage and physical courage. Do you believe that one is more important than the other? Do you believe that one is more difficult than the other?

It took courage for Chandler to make the college decisions she did. Write about what you will take with you – physically and emotionally -- to bolster your courage when you leave home.

In The Wizard of Oz, The Cowardly Lion accompanies Dorothy to the Emerald City to ask for courage. Write about another fictional character and relate his or her story of courage.

It takes courage to stand up for what's right or to try something new. Write about someone – in your life, your school, or even in public life – whose courage you admire.

Find an untold story of courage – big or small. Interview someone from your family, school, or community about an experience that required his or her courage.

About the Author

Chandler DeWitt is currently a student in the Nido R. Qubein School of Communication at High Point University. In her free time, she enjoys playing the guitar, writing, and hanging out with friends.

When she was six years old, her parents founded CWK Network, Inc., Connect with Kids – a multimedia education company that produces Emmy® award-winning television programs and research-based curricula on character and life skills. The U.S. Department of Education has named CWK to its What Works Clearinghouse and describes Connect with Kids as an effective program that improves behavior and attitudes.

Chandler says, "Ever since I can remember, I was the test audience for the latest television program or educational video on the life skill or character trait of the month. Through their work, my parents…have read a lot of research and interviewed hundreds of kids and parents about the pressures that kids face and the choices they make, especially when it comes to drugs, alcohol, sex, the Internet, bullying, and all the other things we hear about in school. I used to roll my eyes and moan when my mom would tell me another one of these stories, but to be honest, I was listening…and more than some of them made me think about things a little differently."

After she graduated from high school, Chandler's parents asked her to consider writing a book about some of the more difficult personal choices she and other teens have to make. They wanted to publish a book from a teenager's perspective – something authentic with an honest point of view. *Inside Out: Real Stories about the Inner Choices That Shape Our Lives* is the result of that effort.

Life Issues & Interests

In addition to addressing 26 nationally recognized character words, all of the Inside Out chapters deal with specific issues facing many pre-teens and teens. Below is an index of topics that will enable you to quickly identify chapters that address specific issues. Beside each topic is the name of the character word(s) associated with the chapter(s) in which you will find the story or stories relating to that topic.

Alcohol	Responsibility, Self-Control, Justice/Fairness
Anger	Peace, Self-Control
Bullying	Civility, Helpfulness
Cyber Bullying	Civility
Cheating	Integrity
Community Involvement	Compassion/Caring, Cooperation
Competition	Honesty, Trustworthiness
Disabilities	Diligence, Patience
Diversity	Kindness, Tolerance
Drinking	Justice/Fairness, Responsibility, Self-Control
Drinking and Driving	Justice/Fairness
Drug Addiction	Freedom
Environment	Cooperation
Family Relationships	Courtesy, Honesty, Honor, Respect, Togetherness
Fine Arts	Conviction, Helpfulness, Loyalty
Friendship	Caring/Compassion, Courtesy, Civility, Kindness, Helpfulness, Trustworthiness

Goal Setting	Honesty, Honor, Perseverance
Learning Differences	Diligence, Perseverance
Lying	Honor
Parent Relationships	Citizenship, Honesty, Honor, Self-Control, Togetherness
Social Relationships	Civility, Courtesy, Helpfulness, Kindness, Trustworthiness
Patriotism	Citizenship, Cooperation
Risk Taking	Citizenship, Courage, Freedom, Honesty, Justice/Fairmess, Patience, Perseverance, Responsibility, Trustworthiness, Self-Control
Self-expression	Conviction, Helpfulness, Loyalty
Shyness	Courage
Sports	Honesty
Teacher Relationships	Conviction, Generosity, Perseverance, Respect
Teamwork	Cooperation
Violence	Peace
Volunteering	Cooperation